Cultural Identity and Political Ethics

Cultural Identity and Political Ethics

PAUL GILBERT

EDINBURGH UNIVERSITY PRESS

© Paul Gilbert, 2010

Edinburgh University Press Ltd
22 George Square, Edinburgh
www.euppublishing.com

Typeset in Palatino by
Servis Filmsetting Ltd, Stockport, Cheshire, and
printed and bound in Great Britain by
CPI Antony Rowe, Chippenham and Eastbourne

A CIP record for this book is available from the British Library

ISBN 978 0 7486 2387 7 (hardback)
ISBN 978 0 7486 2388 4 (paperback)

The right of Paul Gilbert to be identified as author of this work has been
asserted in accordance with the Copyright, Designs and Patents Act
1988.

Acknowledgements

A version of part of Chapter 2 appeared as 'Philosophy, national character, and nationalism' in Guntram H. Herb and David H. Kaplan (eds), *Nations and Nationalism: A Global Historical Overview* (Santa Barbara, CA: ABC-CLIO, 2008) pp. 527–37, and I am grateful for permission to reproduce some of that material here. Chapter 3 is based on a paper given at the University of Rijeka in 2009, part of Chapter 6 on one given at the 'Philosophy and psychoanalysis' conference at the Royal Irish Academy, Dublin, in 2002 and Chapter 7 on my contribution to a symposium in memory of Barrie Falk at the University of Birmingham in 2008. I should like to thank the organisers and participants for the motivation and ideas that these events occasioned. I am grateful to the many colleagues at Hull, past and present, who have provided me with stimulus and suggestions, but most of all to Kathleen Lennon who read several chapters in draft and offered encouragement and criticism. My thanks are due also to Chris Coulson for secretarial assistance, and, by no means least, to Nicola Ramsey and her colleagues at Edinburgh University Press for all their help and patience.

Unless the context indicates otherwise, 'he' and 'she' are used throughout this book without any specific implication as to gender.

Contents

1

The Politics of Identity

The Notion of Cultural Identity

Hermann Goering is credited with saying that whenever he heard the word 'culture' he reached for his revolver. These days, people who reach for revolvers – or heavier weaponry – frequently justify their violent actions by using that word themselves with anything but distaste. For in today's world people's cultural identities are increasingly invoked in support of their political claims. Claims to some form of political recognition for a group on the basis of its members' supposed cultural identity are commonplace, ranging from demands for separate statehood for putatively national groups to an insistence that differences in a multicultural society are acknowledged, and even celebrated, in its political arrangements and processes. This does not apply only to cultural minorities. There is an implied demand, for example, that the shared identity of those who subscribe to 'the values of Western civilisation' should be recognised and protected by political – and military – action. Arguments of a philosophical kind are frequently advanced to justify claims which are grounded in cultural identity. While these vary in detail, many possess a common structure. It is that their cultural identity is of cardinal importance for people, and that this identity is somehow threatened by the withholding of political recognition, the form of which depends upon their circumstances. The value of cultural identity, therefore, allegedly justifies appropriate political recognition of groups whose members share such an identity.

Not all identity politics, of course, concerns cultural identity. Political claims are made in respect of people's identities as black rather than white; women rather than men; as homosexual rather than heterosexual; and so forth. This book is not concerned with these other issues, but this exclusion is not, I believe, just arbitrary. Though there is sometimes talk of black culture or gay culture, what are actually being alluded to in such cases would be better termed 'subcultures'; for they do not cover, as cultures are regarded as doing, a people's whole way of life, but rather a subsection of the activities of some members. For most of the time they participate in the same activities as other members and do so in accordance with the same cultural expectations. The differences which the identities mark are, then, differences within a culture, not differences between cultures. This is a sufficiently important distinguishing feature of cultural identities to treat them separately, since they are, in consequence, freighted with all the importance that culture is meant to have for people.

What, though, is cultural identity? There are, I think, two uses of the notion which need distinguishing. The first is relatively unproblematic. It refers to an individual's identity in its cultural aspects, listing, perhaps, the various features of the way someone has been brought up which identify her in various respects – her linguistic and literary background, her religious and moral education and choices, her socially acquired attitudes and manners and so on. Which broadly cultural features are mentioned will depend upon the context, concerning what marks of distinctiveness or similarity are relevant in it. Thus there should be no suggestion in this case of the notion that there is something

– her socially produced self, as it were – that can be exhaustively specified in terms of such features. How she identifies herself, or how others identify her, in this way is designed to place her, as we say, so that she can be understood and responded to as seems appropriate. An *individual* cultural identity in this sense may well be unique to its possessor, with her particular mix of cultural characteristics; and it is in this sense of cultural identity, I think, that some authors speak of identities as hybrid – the product of cultural mixing.

In a second usage cultural identity refers to membership of a cultural group. It is, therefore, necessarily a *collective* cultural identity, shared by other members of the group. What, though, constitutes a cultural group? It is not simply a group classified in terms of some cultural features or other. If Scousers or Geordies,[1] say, constitute cultural groups, it is not simply because they have distinctive dialects, though these may be the features they are recognised by. It is because such features are taken to mark a range of characteristics across a wide spectrum of life, so that Scousers or Geordies on their home ground can be thought to be fitted to make up a complete society.

The notion of a cultural group, then, is the idea of a group sharing a culture, not just some cultural features. To speak of a culture here is to presuppose that cultural features can be collected together in such a way as to characterise its participants' whole way of life, as this is often expressed, so that one culture can be distinguished globally from another as picking out a distinct way of living. Thus, were Geordies, to make some claims on the basis of their cultural identity as members of such a group, they would be doing more than appealing to their shared dialect, seeking protection for it, say; they would be appealing to some more substantial commonality – their supposed way of life, perhaps – as what needed to be safeguarded. We have already seen in distinguishing subcultures from cultures how the latter notion functions to take in an indefinitely wide range of activities. The idea of cultural identity as membership of a cultural group therefore involves the idea of such a supposedly wide-ranging identity.

I have tried briefly to explain, then, how I shall be using the notion of cultural identity in what follows. My choice of usage is not arbitrary. It matches, I believe, the use made of the notion by those who invoke it in support of various political claims. For these claims are made on behalf of groups supposedly constituted by cultural features which are shared by their members and which, in an important respect, make them the people that they are; that is to say, confer on them these identities because they are members of such groups. It is since these groups are in this sense identity groups that their claims have the kind of prima facie force that they do. These cultural identities are, furthermore, taken to be fairly all embracing, so that invoking them calls forth a conception of their bearers as people differing from others not just in some small number of obvious respects, but in how quite generally they conceive their lives. Thus, although there is a continuum of claims supported by such invocations, what stands as the exemplary limiting case is the claim to be able to live an entirely separate life. By what criterion of a common culture this is facilitated is a matter on which political leaders – and philosophers – differ, and we shall later go on to examine contrasting criteria appealed to in identifying distinct cultural groups.

I should add, though, at this point that a cultural group should not necessarily be thought of as a community, in at least the sense of a group of people actually leading a common life. The widespread assimilation of cultural groups to cultural communities emphasises again, I think, the assumption among those who think of themselves as members of such a group that they do share wide-ranging features which could enable them to form a community. But this is not to say that they actually do form one, however much they might wish they did. In the circumstances in which they find themselves they may not have the sort of interactions between themselves that are needed for this, while in fact having just such interactions with members of other groups, so that if there is any community they are part of, then it is a multicultural one. Cultural identity should not be thought of as communal identity, therefore, in the sense of some identity I have in virtue of my relationships to other members of a group leading a common life – by analogy, perhaps, with my identity as a family member. If cultural and communal identities do correspond, they are still separate and differently constituted identities.

Identity in Practice and Theory

Claims made on the basis of one's identity seem to have an especial potency. How can one possibly be denied what is due to one in virtue of who one is? One has a claim to the plane seat indicated by the boarding card with one's own name on it – a much stronger claim than that of the passenger who simply prefers a window seat. And if the trespassing passenger truculently asks, 'How do I know it is your seat?' one has a right to be recognised as the person one is, which one may enforce by brandishing a passport or other identity document with one's name and photo on it. Such a document will typically also show one's sex, date and place of birth and, of course, one's nationality. For official purposes one is the national of that name, sex and origin, an identity established for practical purposes by features of one's physical appearance.

In this example, one's claim derives from an allocation of rights made merely on the basis of who one is, not on the basis of any further properties. The properties itemised in one's documentation simply serve to individuate one; they do not provide reasons why the allocation has been made as it has. If, by contrast, one has been invited to the conference to which one is flying on the basis of being the author of such and such books, then it is as that author that one is attending, and being that author provides the reason for one's invitation. It is as that author that I am introduced to the other delegates and being that author serves as my only relevant identity for the duration of the conference. When I return home to the bosom of my family neither of the above identities, one would hope, is pertinent to who I am. Here I am that familiar individual who is my wife's husband, my son's father, and so forth. The claims I make on them, which are closely connected with my occupying these roles, stem rather, for the most part, from my being the person with that domestic history.

But which, someone may ask, is my *real* identity? Tempting as it may be to suppose that one's familial identity is somehow more basic than one's professional or official one, it is not clear that there is any sense to the notion of an identity which one has outside of a particular context. One's identity is the way in which one identifies oneself to others or is identified by them. One is likely to attach more importance to the context in which one identifies oneself to one's family than to those in which one identifies oneself professionally or in the bare terms of one's official identity. That is why it is the familial identity which seems to capture both more of what one is and what is more fundamental to who one is than do these other identities. But there seems to be no identity one can give which somehow conveys who one is irrespective of the context. Asked out of the blue, as it were, 'Who are you?' the right, if suspicious sounding, reply may well be, 'What do you want to know for?' For until one knows the context of the question one has no idea how to answer it, what it is about one that the questioner wishes to know.

Collective identities share these features with individual ones. A collective identity gives one answer to the question 'Who are you (plural)?' otherwise than by giving a list of individual identities. Thus it may also be alluded to in response to a 'Who are you (singular)?' question, when only the collectivity to which one belongs is requested, not any characteristic that marks one out from the others comprising that collectivity. Nationality is an obvious example. One may, for instance, be allocated to one queue at passport control desks, rather than another even more interminable one on the basis of having a European Union nationality as against a non-EU identity. The allocation here, as in the plane seat case, is made simply on the basis of one's relevant collective identity. While no doubt I must satisfy certain tests to qualify for this identity, there is nothing about the identity that provides a reason for my having a place in one queue, the shorter one, rather than in another, as, say, being old and infirm might furnish a reason for getting through more quickly.

Yet the idea of a bare collective identity supporting a claim is, I suggest, more common than the writings of political theorists might suggest. The system of official national identities provides a framework for it. Thus the nationals of a country are allocated that country's territory as their rightful residence. Their claim to it may derive solely from this fact. That they should be allocated any country as theirs or that they should be allocated this particular country are matters for which reasons may be sought but for which their bare national identities provide none. The existence of this system of allocation, however, may sometimes be enough to explain such facts as the resident nationals' resentment of immigration, in which those not allocated places, so to speak, take them. No facts about their cultural incompatibility with established residents or their effect on the residents' culture seem to be required. So far, only the existence of the system needs to be appealed to to support claims based on official identities or supposedly to counter claims unsupported by them.

Things are different when we turn to situations in which

groups are unhappy with the system for a variety of reasons, in particular when the official identities it ascribes them do not entitle them to the allocation they desire. It is then that they may deny that their official identity is their real one. In a context changed from that of formal compliance to one of political protest, they demand that some other identity be recognised as theirs, with a view to it becoming their official identity and to corresponding alterations in the system of allocation. How this other identity is selected will, I shall argue, depend upon the political circumstances and the political objectives to be achieved. But what, in general terms, such a supposed identity group must deny is that the system of allocation is simply arbitrary. For it to lay claim to a place in the system currently denied it, the group must provide a reason why it should be treated like other groups which have such a place. That is to say it must claim that there is no morally relevant difference between it and these other groups. But this presupposes that there is some reason why they occupy that place, a reason of a kind which it shares.

This, I suggest, is the general form of many nationalist claims, separatist or irredentist, and indeed that of other recognition claims from minority groups. These will usually be supported in terms of an alleged cultural identity, with reference to one or other of the different criteria which we shall distinguish. Which kind of cultural identity is asserted will depend upon many factors. It may be the same kind as that of a dominant group from which a minority seeks separation, on grounds of a distinct language, religion or other feature, as in the case of Kurdish separatists in Turkey. It may be a different kind, as when a common language criterion, say, is borrowed from another putative nation state to support an independence claim against a multilingual state which utilises no such criterion, and which is, therefore, thought of by opponents as culturally ill formed, as with Québecois secessionists. In these sorts of political contexts the way the group identifies itself depends upon the pattern of inclusion and exclusion which they seek to formalise, and which is likely to reflect one of a number of pre-existing patterns of social difference. Yet outside the context of particular political claims or presumptions it is not apparent that there is anything than can count as one's cultural identity, in the sense in which this is appealed to in support of such claims.

This kind of conclusion is going to seem intolerably sceptical. Surely one's cultural identity cannot be whatever cultural membership one has that can be utilised to support certain political claims? Yet the notion of identity involved here is no less a political concept than the notion of a nationality, as recorded on passports and the like, is an official one, which tells us very little about a person. But there is every political reason for attaching a great deal more importance to it, since the more significant it is in a person's life the stronger the support it provides for the political claims based upon it. We shall need, then, to investigate the idea of collective cultural identity as it is used in such political contexts to see if there really is a deeper notion of identity that can be drawn upon there than the tactical one our sceptical story has sketched out.

Communitarian philosophers like Charles Taylor[2] have, in recent years, provided theoretical support for the kinds of claim that political leaders have lodged in the name of their followers' cultural identities. Although such philosophers frequently make the assimilation of cultural groups to communities which I warned against earlier, one way of taking their basic thesis is that individuals are what they are only because they are 'embedded' in cultures. They are not asocial atoms, as it were, whose cultural characteristics are detachable from them. Rather, they are defined by these characteristics. The thesis is not, therefore, simply a genetic one about the effects of socialisation; it is a metaphysical thesis about what people are. If we add to the idea that cultural characteristics comprise a range of resources upon which individuals can draw in living their lives the assumption that these resources come packaged into fairly discrete bounded cultures, then the strong conclusion follows that what makes someone who she is is her embeddedness in some particular culture. A refusal duly to recognise this culture then seemingly amounts to denigration of, or even a threat to, her identity.

It has not only been communitarians who have elicited political conclusions from related views about people's cultural embeddedness. Liberals too, of various stamps, have avowed forms of 'culturalism', arguing either that people's self-respect requires recognition of their cultural groups or that their capacity for autonomous choice is possible only within a secure culture. One type of liberal culturalism, adopted in different ways by Yael Tamir[3] and by Will Kymlicka,[4] involves supporting claims for national self-determination for one or other of the above reasons, given that nations are a kind of cultural group. Kymlicka himself draws a distinction between the nations to which indigenous people belong and which have complete cultures, and immigrant groups which have only a limited range of cultural characteristics and to which he accords more restricted cultural rights. Other liberals who reject such a distinction might correspondingly resist nationalism in favour of a multiculturalism which gives equal recognition to what are seen as a multiplicity of cultural groups within a society.

A similar conclusion is drawn from different premises by philosophers who reject liberalism as a framework for thinking about the politics of cultural identity. One reason for doing so, advanced by Bhikhu Parekh[5] for example, is that liberalism is a doctrine specific to a particular culture and hence inapt for assessing the claims of different cultural identities. Others, like Iris Marion Young,[6] repudiate liberalism on feminist grounds, seeing it as imposing an inappropriately general conception of citizenship to which equal recognition admits people. Here too, though, there are differences between those, like Parekh, who see cultural groups as relatively clear cut and others, like Young, who discern only layers of heterogeneity in which cultural identity, as we are understanding it, has no special priority over other identities. Nevertheless, Young's advocacy of group representation in political systems would, it appears, have the effect of according a type of recognition to cultural groups in order to overcome inequalities of political inclusion.

Young adopts a version of the deliberative democracy model in which political claims on behalf of cultural groups, among others, should be settled by mutual negotiation, and a similar position is taken by Seyla Benhabib[7] who advocates multicultural dialogue. Such deliberation can even be urged as determining what form cultural recognition itself might take, as it is by Matthew Festenstein.[8] All such accounts assume that people enter the political sphere in their cultural identities, whether or not by formal means such as group representation. This is itself to concede a form of recognition of distinct cultural identities, in however complex or indeterminate a way these are conceived. From a wide spectrum of starting points, then, a politics of cultural identity has received philosophical endorsement and support, surprisingly perhaps, in view of the political disruption and violent conflict to which such an identity politics has given rise.

This view has not, of course, gone unopposed. The most influential attack has come from Brian Barry[9] who argues against a wide range of cultural rights claims on the grounds that the recognition of cultural identities is incompatible with equality, in particular with liberal equality in civil and political rights. One of his special targets, in consequence, is James Tully[10] who has argued that different cultural groups should be free to govern themselves in accordance with their own rules and customs. Barry, by contrast, argues for precisely the 'identical basket of rights' that Taylor proclaims as failing to 'recognise . . . the unique identity of this individual or group, their distinctness from everyone else'.[11] And the basis for these rights, in Barry's view, is an egalitarian liberalism.

Other liberals too have opposed a politics of cultural identity. Chandran Kukathas[12] has consistently criticised Kymlicka's view that cultural identities need to be recognised through granting groups differentiated rights and that this is consistent with – indeed demanded by – liberalism. Instead Kukathas urges freedom of association as a more important liberal value than autonomy, so that there is, as he puts it, a 'cultural market place' in which the state should not interfere, neither to 'promote nor inhibit the maintenance of any particular culture'[13] by granting specific cultural rights. Jacob Levy[14] draws similar conclusions from rather different, though, as he sees it, still liberal premises. The job of the state is, Levy believes, to secure its members against the threat of ethnic violence and the like. This requires conceding the importance of cultural identities while questioning their value, and consequently not according general recognition to cultural groups. Levy argues, in particular, against liberal nationalism, adopting arguments I have myself advanced for the impossibility of recognising all putative nations because of their conflicting criteria of membership.[15]

An attack on the politics of cultural identity from a rather different direction, though also a part of Barry's critique, is that it is inconsistent with a politics of redistribution. One version of this view is a radical cosmopolitanism which sees the restricted loyalties implicit in cultural identifications – particularly national ones – as incompatible with the justice due to all human beings. Other, more limited positions regard the recognition of identities as blurring the underlying economic and social reasons that lie behind claims for it. Thus Nancy Fraser[16] argues that what really needs to be recognised is the equal status of members of disadvantaged groups which has to do, not with the self-respect of a secure identity, as Taylor and those who follow him suppose, but with the dignity that comes from equal participation in social life. In this way Fraser seeks to reconcile cultural recognition, understood in her way, with redistribution.

Finally, in this brief overview, we should mention some more fundamental criticisms of the assumptions underlying philosophical defences of the politics of cultural identity. While philosophers influenced by feminism, like Young, Benhabib and others, are anxious to criticise what they view as the reification and essentialism involved in thinking of cultural groups as fairly discrete, bounded wholes, Jeremy Waldron[17] has attacked not only the supposed unity of cultures in contemporary circumstances but the value alleged for this by Kymlicka and others as conducive to autonomy. Perhaps even more radical is Richard Rorty's[18] refusal to allow an appeal to any metaphysical notions, like that of the culturally embedded self, to add anything by way of support to political claims. Yet Rorty is content to argue for such claims on the basis of liberal principles, 'ethnocentric' as he admits they are.

What the present book aims to do is to join the assault on the politics of cultural identity, but to do so without espousing any of the various theoretical positions – liberalism in some form, cosmopolitanism or whatever – from which it is generally launched. While all of these suggest solutions to the political problems posed by claims for cultural recognition, as do those taken by philosophers sympathetic to it, this is not the purpose of this book. It is, rather, to scrutinise the foundations of a politics of cultural identity and on that basis to urge scepticism about its claims.

I start by looking at the origins of ideas like that of cultural identity in German Romantic thought and their manifestation in notions of national character. Like cultural identity, national character was thought of as a deep-going feature of individual psychology and it is with a critique of this conception that much of the book is concerned. I suggest that it is also a mistake to view cultural identity as a uniform phenomenon. Rather, different types of cultural identity emerge in response to different sorts of circumstance with which groups of people are confronted. In all these cases, though, it is surface features of behaviour that mark out distinct identities rather than deep psychological differences. Furthermore, I set out to show these surface features as having a principally aesthetic appeal, through evoking which, cultural identities are constructed. Finally, I argue that the political employment of the notion of cultural identity is in several respects morally pernicious. A different kind of politics might have avoided its problems and deceits, but perhaps it is too late to hope for one.

Notes

1. Scousers are inhabitants of Liverpool, Geordies of Newcastle.
2. See especially, Charles Taylor, *Multiculturalism: Examining the Politics of Recognition* (Princeton, NJ: Princeton University Press, 1994).
3. Yael Tamir, *Liberal Nationalism* (Princeton, NJ: Princeton University Press, 1993).
4. For example, Will Kymlicka, *Multicultural Citizenship: a Liberal Theory of Minority Rights* (Oxford: Oxford University Press, 1995).
5. Bhikhu Parekh, *A New Politics of Identity: Political Principles for an Interdependent World* (Basingstoke: Palgrave Macmillan, 2008), pp. 117–21.
6. Iris Marion Young, *Justice and the Politics of Difference* (Princeton, NJ: Princeton University Press, 1990).
7. Seyla Benhabib, *The Claims of Culture: Equality and Diversity in a Global Era* (Princeton, NJ: Princeton University Press, 2002).
8. Matthew Festenstein, *Negotiating Diversity: Culture, Deliberation, Trust* (Cambridge: Polity, 2005).
9. Brian Barry, *Culture and Equality* (Cambridge: Polity, 2001).
10. James Tully, *Strange Multiplicity: Constitutionalism in an Age of Diversity* (Cambridge: Cambridge University Press, 1995).
11. Charles Taylor, *Philosophical Arguments* (Cambridge, MA: Harvard University Press, 1995), p. 234.

12. Chandran Kukathas, *The Liberal Archipelago* (Oxford: Oxford University Press, 2003).
13. Ibid. p. 14.
14. Jacob Levy, *The Multiculturalism of Fear* (Oxford: Oxford University Press, 2000).
15. Paul Gilbert, *The Philosophy of Nationalism* (Boulder, CO: Westview, 1998), esp. p. 173.
16. Nancy Fraser, 'Rethinking recognition', *New Left Review*, 3 (2000), pp. 107–20.
17. Jeremy Waldron, 'Minority cultures and the cosmopolitan alternative', in W. Kymlicka (ed.), *The Rights of Minority Cultures* (Oxford: Oxford University Press, 1995).
18. Richard Rorty, 'The priority of democracy to philosophy', in Richard Rorty, *Objectivity, Relativism and Truth* (Cambridge: Cambridge University Press, 1991).

2
National Character

Character and Identity

The most apparently novel ideas are seldom without their historical precedents, though their connection with these is usually concealed. Thus the politics of identity that has come to the fore within the last twenty years overturns a half century of thinking in which what was supposedly the same across all people determined the political agenda: how could people, supposedly much the same, best be organised and governed? The politics of identity indicates, instead, a range of differences between people and asks how such differences can best be accommodated politically and socially. There are many types of difference involved here, of course, in particular, differences of gender, occluded in what was taken to be a previously male-orientated political problematic. But cultural identity, including *national* identity, has assumed a special contemporary importance, not least because of its manifest potential for a kind and degree of conflict more threatening than that arising from other types of difference. Yet cultural identity, I suggest, recapitulates in many respects, though not all, the role played by national character in dominating the agenda of international politics from two hundred years ago until the clash of universalist visions that characterised the Cold War.

Once upon a time it was thought that we all shared a common human nature – a nature that lay at the bottom of our understanding of each other's actions. Or at least those in the educated West thought so. Those outside might have had darker thoughts. For in eighteenth-century Europe this picture formed part of that secularised version of the Christian message of love and hope for mankind which we call the Enlightenment. It finds a classic expression in David Hume: 'Mankind are so much the same in all times and places that history informs us of nothing new or strange',[1] and Hume's whole philosophy is predicated upon such a view. It is a picture which inspired Enlightenment projects of liberalism, socialism and, of course, cosmopolitanism. Nor has it lost its resonance today. At the end of the eighteenth century, however, a counter-Enlightenment movement emerged with a contrasting image of human beings and the explanation of their actions. It reached back to the observations of the ancients on the apparently radical differences between the various peoples they encountered and to the causes to which these differences were attributed by philosophers.

The idea that different peoples have different characters and consequentially different kinds of state was a commonplace among the Greeks. Plato notes that

> there is a difference in places . . . and some beget better men and others worse; and we must legislate accordingly. Some places are subject to strange and fatal influences by reason of diverse winds and violent heats, some by reason of waters; or again from the character of that subsistence which the earth supplies them, which not only affects the bodies of men for good or evil, but produces similar results in their souls.[2]

Aristotle follows this climatic explanation of such differences by crediting 'the nations that live in cold regions and those of Europe' with spirit but a relative lack of skill and intellect, while the reverse is true of the 'Asiatic nations'. This leads to the former being free but lacking political cohesion while the latter are 'enslaved and subject'.[3] And there are differences in the relative intellect and courage of the different Greek nations.

Largely it is to the Greeks, then, that we originally owe this idea of very different kinds of people in different places, people differing in their natures. But the notion of nature here is ambiguous as between potentiality and achievement, between, as we may say in the human case, personality and character. The resort to climatic explanations of difference suggests the latter idea. Peoples differ in their characters – in the ways they feel and act – which have been formed by external factors, not necessarily in personalities formed internally which provide their potential for displaying such traits. Thus if we associate the notion of racial difference with a story of internal biologically produced difference then this is not the Greek conception, notwithstanding Plato's insistence on the importance of breeding desirable characteristics into people as into animals. What is important to the Greeks is the view that the differences that exist between peoples are ones that are relevant to the way they are, or should be, governed.

We can contrast this with the Roman view that the same kind of political life in the same polity is satisfactory for anyone. Whatever differences there are between them, these are not politically relevant. For, given the appropriate territorial qualifications and allegiance, all free men are candidates for citizenship of the same polity. The differences, then, are relevant neither to the form of polity nor to its boundaries. There is, of course, a parallel to this in the Christian story. St Augustine, writing shortly after the sack of Rome, sees entry to the City of God as open to all believing human beings. The earthly city, by contrast, is in no similar way a single polity, divided into different communities according to the different objects of their members' love. But these improper objects of love are, by grace, replaceable through true belief. There is nothing about the kinds of peoples that there are that divides them into groups that should be governed separately or otherwise treated differently as members of a polity. And it is, as I hinted, a secularised version of this conception, with strong Roman undercurrents, that characterises the Enlightenment.

It is to the counter-Enlightenment thinker Johann Gottfried von Herder that the modern revival of the ancient Greek politics of difference is largely due, and it was he who was mainly responsible for the German intellectual discovery of Greek thought. Herder has thus bequeathed us a picture of human variety and its political implications which is now surely the dominant one, even when co-existing uneasily with its Enlightenment predecessor. For Herder writes that

> every region of the earth has its peculiar species of animals which cannot live elsewhere, and consequently must have been born in it, why should it not have its own kind of men? Are not the varieties of natural features, manners and character, and particularly the great differences in language proof of this? . . . The Arab of the desert belongs to it, as much as his noble horse and his patient indefatigable camel.[4]

Herder concludes, in anti-universalist vein, that different nations need to be governed separately, in accordance with systems and laws that suit their national characters. Anything else leads to what he terms 'artificial constructions', which end, Herder maintains, in disorder and disaster.

The first modern manifestation of Herderian ideas is nationalism. 'An actual nation consists,' writes Henry Sidgwick in 1891, 'of persons of whom the predominant number have . . . a certain vaguely defined complex of particular characteristics which we call the "national character" of Englishmen, Frenchmen, etc.'⁵ Sidgwick is following John Stuart Mill writing earlier. 'That alone which . . . enables any body of human beings to exist as a society,' he claims, 'is national character . . . A philosophy of laws and institutions, not founded on a philosophy of national character, is an absurdity.'⁶ It is this notion of national character which is such a pervasive feature of nationalism in the nineteenth century and the first half of the twentieth. It is shared national character which comes to be taken as individuating all nations, although this apparently uniform criterion is deceptive. Yet the notion plays a key role in nationalist ideologies of the period as they apply both to established states and to peoples seeking national secession or reunification.

Nationalism may be taken to be the belief that there are groups of people – 'nations' – united in such a way that they possess a right of shared and separate statehood, other things being equal. The problem for nationalists is to specify what this uniting feature is and why it generates this right. Notoriously, a wide range of answers have been given to this question, leading to difficulties for theorists in providing a single account of what a nation is. The French thinker Ernest Renan's celebrated paper 'What is a nation?', written in 1882, runs through a range of suggested criteria: race, language, religion, common interests and geography; and he dismisses them all as either unnecessary, as shown by counter examples, or insufficient. His own account is, famously, that 'the existence of a nation is . . . a daily plebiscite',⁷ expressing a people's continued common will to live together. On the face of it this represents a different movement of thought from that which postulates a shared national character. But even this is potentially misleading. For, although Renan explains the common will that generates a right to statehood as deriving from recognition of a shared history, he glosses this thus: 'The Spartan song "We are what ye were, and we should be what ye are," is, in its simplicity, the abridged version of every national anthem.'[8] One way of making this identification with past members of the nation is through the invocation of a shared national character, as manifest, for example, in the figures of national history.

This, then, is the first role of national character: to secure the identification with other members of the nation, past and present, from those for whom a common national identity is claimed. They recognise themselves in the valorised descriptions of the character or aspire to so recognise themselves. Thus, writing in 1917, the novelist Somerset Maugham remarks:

> Every nation forms for itself a type to which it accords its admiration . . . It is an ideal to which writers of fiction seek to give body and substance. The characteristics which they ascribe to this figment of their fancy are those which the nation at a given moment aspires to, and presently simple men, fascinated by these creatures of fiction, take them as their model and actually transform themselves, so that you may recognise in real life a type which you have seen described in novels.[9]

Conversely, however, members of the nation distance themselves from the character traits which they ascribe to members of other nations, which are commonly represented in uncomplimentary terms.

The second role of national character is to provide a ground for loyalty and partiality. Merely to have a shared national character may not yet seem to generate a people's right to statehood, but their loyalty to their nation and preparedness to give preferential treatment to it and to its members over others may suggest a reason why they should share a state, namely that the political obligations which it imposes will then mirror, rather than conflict with, the national obligations which they freely undertake. A possible ground for national partiality is that one's fellow members possess valuable character traits, in particular in that they are pursuing values one shares oneself, so that in giving them support one is furthering those values and expressing the associated character traits oneself. By contrast, members of other nations lacking these traits and values are relatively undeserving. While this line of argument is of dubious cogency, it does account for much nationalist thinking, especially if combined with a view of a nation's mission and of the particular fittingness of its members to fulfil it in virtue of their national character – a combination of views common in the period and which we shall explore shortly.

The third role of national character is to provide a justification for a political right, namely the right to statehood, either indirectly via the above line of argument or more directly through the idea that those with a common character are apt for shared government in a way that those with divergent temperaments are not. The kind of laws that suit people who want a quiet life, for example, would be different from those appropriate to those of a more noisy and excitable disposition. But, in addition to these aptness considerations entitlement claims might be proffered, if character is seen to involve the pursuit of particular values. For now, it might be suggested, national self-determination is only an extension of personal self-determination – the right to live one's life in accordance with one's own values. In the collective case this may only be possible if one can utilise the political organisation of a state.

Yet an appeal to national character offers a preferable justification of the right to statehood to the grounds for it which Renan considers and rejects – race, language, religion, and so on. For the difficulty with these is that they generate different and conflicting claims. The common language criterion which shaped Yugoslavia, for example, was always under challenge by the mainly religious criteria that separate Croats and Serbs. Yet if a claim to statehood is to carry conviction it must employ the same criterion as is used by others. Shared national character purports to provide a common yardstick for identifying nations and acknowledging their political rights. This is, like the foregoing considerations, a rational reconstruction of the place of character in nationalist ideology. It was, and it remains, philosophically under-theorised. Nevertheless, there are philosophical supports for this feature of nationalism which we shall go on to explore.

But why, we may ask, should the idea deriving from the Greeks that the people of different places have different characters lead to the notion that there are distinct *national* characters – lead, that is, to the view that these differences of character follow national lines rather than, say, more local ones? A socio-historical explanation can no doubt be offered in terms of the need, from the latter part of the nineteenth century onwards, to mobilise mass support for nation states or for national movements, and we have seen how an appeal to national character might achieve this. But a *justification* for the appeal will require us to consider, in the next section, what accounts of the formation of national character might be offered. Meanwhile, we need to look at two more general philosophical considerations affecting the invocation of character as individuating nations.

The first is, of course, the doctrine enunciated by Jean-Jacques Rousseau that a state is legitimate if, and only if, its people are sovereign within it. This leads immediately to the question, 'Who are the people?' If our interest in asking it is to arrive at a system of legitimate states then there are two prima facie rather different ways of addressing it. One is to see, with Renan, what groups of people share a common will to live together, which yields what we can call the subjectivist answer. This exploits the current of modern thought in which human beings are represented as essentially rational calculators, able to determine how to achieve happiness individually and collectively. The other way exploits a different current, which is to see peoples as sharing certain human needs but differing naturally or culturally. This objectivist approach identifies the peoples whose sovereignty would legitimise states as categories picked out by differences which make them apt for separate statehood. Here the anthropological observations that accompanied late nineteenth-century colonialism as well as the study of European folk cultures, differing more than those of elites, exercised an influence. Indeed, in the former case they were used to justify imperialism on the grounds that colonised peoples lacked the psychological attributes required for exercising sovereignty, while in the latter they served to challenge existing empires by discerning large differences between ordinary people who were then recruited to independence movements.

Although in the earlier nineteenth century the subjectivist approach was dominant, in the latter part the objectivist takes over. But the notion of national character is able, to some extent, to span the two. The reason for this is that, in the philosophical psychology of the time, character is seen as the seat of the volitions. 'Character,' writes William McDougall in 1908, 'has been defined as that from which the will proceeds'; and will might equally well be defined as 'that which proceeds from character'.[10] Thus, on an objectivist view, national character can be seen as that which gives rise to a common will, particularly if, as in McDougall, an 'attraction of like to like' is postulated as underlying 'the more definite ethical and political groupings'.[11] Conversely, on a subjectivist account, a common national character can be attributed on the basis of a coincidence of wills, since this must indicate a sharing of the values which are the determinants of character. The emphasis on character, therefore, allows apparent differences as to who a sovereign people might be to be obscured by postulating a nomic correspondence between national will and national character traits.

The second philosophical consideration which explains the invocation of character is its importance in the ethics of the period. The popular influence of the notion, not only in Victorian Britain, may be gauged by the fact that Samuel Smiles's *Character*, published in 1871, was reprinted no less that twenty-seven times before the turn of the century and continued in circulation well into the middle of the next. 'The same qualities which determine the character of individuals,' he remarks, 'also determine the character of nations',[12] so character building evidently has a national benefit. However, there are at least two distinct philosophical reasons why one might emphasise the importance of character. Throughout the late nineteenth and earlier twentieth century utilitarianism remained an important theory of ethics. But utilitarianism both seems to run counter to common sense and to render the making of moral judgements inordinately difficult. The nineteenth-century resolution of these problems by philosophers like Henry Sidgwick was to regard the character traits commonly regarded as valuable as those that are felicific in generally leading to actions that produce the greatest happiness, so that those who display them simply follow their virtuous dispositions in deciding how to act.

There was, however, another distinct but influential theory of philosophical ethics which makes the measure of the goodness of an act not its consequences but the very fact that it displays virtuous motives and thus an admirable character. For example, F. H. Bradley's idealist ethics holds that man's ultimate end is self-realisation, but that the self to be realised is principally that of the social organism to which someone belongs, since 'he is what he is, in brief, so far as he is what others also are'.[13] Thus insofar as he acts in accordance with his community's moral self he tends to act well, since this will express the sort of unity which constitutes a man's character, by contrast with acting from disorganised instincts. Bradley admits that one may have to look beyond one's own community, which may be to some extent corrupt; yet it is evident how this view of ethics naturally allies itself with the valorisation of national character as that to which one should aspire to conform.

Character Formation

Different nationalisms, we noticed earlier, depend upon different criteria for what they take to be their nation – race, religion, language, and so forth. The way these different criteria connect with an apparently uniform conception of national character is by providing different accounts of its formation. One is not, of course, obliged to refer to only one causal factor. Reflecting upon national character in 1927, the political philosopher and historian Ernest Barker lists three 'material factors' – race, geography and economy – and four 'spiritual' ones – politics, religion, language and education – seeing all of them as contributing to shaping it.[14] His curious neglect of history as a factor is perhaps to be explained by his regarding the formative process as itself historical. But Barker does not appreciate the political point of seizing upon a single criterion, or a small set of them, namely that this is the one that applies to the group for whom a right to statehood is claimed. In these circumstances one kind of account of the formation of its national character, rather than another, will be forced upon the group's nationalists. What is more, an appropriate philosophical underpinning for this kind of account of its formation will be forced upon them too.

It would be an oversimplification to regard the late nineteenth and earlier twentieth century as a battleground between materialist and idealist metaphysics, and even more so to see Barker's material and spiritual factors captured by the former and the latter respectively. Nonetheless, it is worth bearing this crude picture in mind in considering what follows. For we shall go on to look at various philosophical frameworks to see what accounts they can offer for national character, and we shall notice to what nationalisms, and hence to what purportedly national groups, they are congenial or not, as the case may be. The theoretical situation is, however, complex, with the materialist/idealist distinction not necessarily following the objectivist/subjectivist one mentioned earlier. The latter contrast finds expression, in one of its forms, in Friedrich Meinecke's 1907 distinction between the cultural and the political nation.[15] It is usually assumed that the political nation corresponds to that envisaged by liberal nationalists as against culturalist authoritarian ones. But again this is over simple, not least because liberals, following John Stuart Mill, tended to assume that people's desire to associate would follow along lines of cultural affinity. In sum, it is impossible here to do more than provide a few examples of philosophical lines of thought influencing the way particular nationalists conceptualised their national groups in terms of the formation of their national characters.

One influential strand of materialist philosophy is social Darwinism, though Herbert Spencer, who may be considered its most influential exponent, had adumbrated his principle of evolution by which only the fittest survive, prior to Darwin's *Origin of Species* and with none of Darwin's scientific method. Spencer is thus naturally drawn in his *Man Versus the State* of 1884 to a libertarian position in which government properly exists solely for the enforcement of contracts, to which he elsewhere adds the maintenance of security through war. But Spencer also believed that people came together in a social organism which grows rather than being made and thus again needs to be left to its own devices to flourish or to perish. Spencer's ideas were carried forward in Benjamin Kidd's *Social Evolution* of 1894, which explicitly presents rivalry between individuals, societies, nations and races as the mechanism whereby the fittest in each category come to the fore. This sort of thinking sees character – individual, national or racial – as operative here, the impulsiveness of Bushmen, according to Spencer, unfitting them for the social union through which progress is possible. It issues in Karl Pearson's *National Life and Character*, appearing in the same year as Kidd's book, and Pearson advocates war with 'inferior races' and competition with 'equal' ones for economic advantage.

Social Darwinism regards national character as largely an inherited characteristic, shaped in a rivalrous struggle for existence. Its maintenance and improvement therefore depends principally upon eugenic methods and the vanquishing of opponents. The latter militarist conclusion was exposed by Norman Angell's eponymous volume of 1909 as 'The Great Illusion', since, he argues, it is the fittest who go to war and they perish rather than survive. The former strategy was generally seen as one of preserving racial purity, although Spencer himself believed that mixing similar stocks will derive the evolved advantages of both. While this sort of eugenic thinking affected most Western countries during the period, each advertising their own national characters as best fitted for survival, it was notoriously in German nationalism and Nazi supranational racism that its most baneful effects were encountered.

Germany had long had a racist tradition of thinking about its national character originating in the fifteenth-century discovery of Tacitus's *Germania* and its portrayal of Germans as morally admirable because racially pure. Despite his insistence on the will as shaping individual character, Kant has a physiological view of temperament as manifest in inherited national and racial characters. Kant compares these on an evaluative scale, the German coming out best, unlike Herder who sees them as simply best fitted to their different conditions. Fichte, however, also sees the Germans as a superior people, though there is a crucial twist in his argument as to why they are. Certainly they are a racially pure 'primordial' people, but what accounts for their moral superiority is that, unlike other Teutonic peoples, they continue to speak their original uncontaminated language – the criterion, Fichte thinks, following Herder, of German national identity. This enables them to understand the thoughts it expresses in a way that speakers of languages that are introduced or have introduced elements cannot. Yet, as Elie Kedourie observes, 'there is no clear-cut distinction between linguistic and racial nationalism . . . a nation's language was peculiar to that nation only because such a nation constituted a racial stock distinct from other nations',[16] and he goes on to cite the French fascist Charles Maurras as holding that Jews were unable to understand French as Frenchmen proper can. One cannot, therefore, become a member of a nation by learning its language. It was in this racialised form that linguistic nationalism percolated through Europe and could thus be combined with elements of social Darwinism.

The most notorious example in this period of a philosopher embracing racist nationalism is Martin Heidegger, whose inaugural address as rector of Freiburg University in 1933[17] borrows themes from Fichte's *Address to the German People* a century and a quarter earlier. Like Fichte, Heidegger sees himself as speaking at a moment of crisis in which the German people are under threat, while at the same time their position as primordial people at the centre of Europe gives them a special mission. It is a mission they are uniquely able to discharge because of the peculiar properties of the language they are given – a language which, like many languages, necessarily shapes their thought and action. But the German language's transparency to thought especially fits it for the original metaphysical thinking required to resolve the crisis by providing a ground for the new German political order – a grounding achieved in Nietzschean mode, through a fundamental questioning of received assumptions, rather than by a restatement of established values. As a starting point Heidegger urges a return to the pre-Socratics, particularly Heraclitus, whose dark saying that 'war is common and justice is conflict, and everything comes about in accordance with conflict and necessity',[18] provides a justification for similar attitudes to the social Darwinism which, as a philosophical system, Heidegger would have rejected. While Heidegger's ideas had little or no influence on nationalism, the difficulty is to divine whether features of his more general philosophical system might conduce to acceptance of it or other objectionable forms of identity politics.

The same question can be raised about the idealism that originates in the work of Hegel and which continued to exercise an influence in the late nineteenth and early twentieth century. Indeed, it was defences of German nationalism in this idealist spirit to which Heidegger was opposed, though, looking back on the phenomenon in 1945, Karl Popper credits Hegel – probably unfairly – with fathering the 'new tribalism' it expressed.[19] Yet certainly a Hegelian philosophy of history that sees world events as the unfolding of spirit, and individual nations, through their members' national characters, as playing a part in this development, leads directly to a conception of national mission that is potentially dangerous, particularly when allied to Hegel's doctrine that war preserves the ethical health of a nation. Ideas like these were taken up and they present a picture of the formation of national character little different from, though even more mysterious than, that of social Darwinism. But are there not more benign forms of idealism which dispense with the worst of them?

Bernard Bosanquet's idealist work, *The Philosophical Theory of the State*, exerted considerable influence in Britain. In his introduction to a third edition in 1919 he writes:

'England' has always meant the cause of humanity; so has every nation, so far as it saw and fought for a true good. All saw the good differently; in the house of humanity are many mansions; but all saw some of it, not in themselves alone, and knew darkly that they were there to see it and to champion it.[20]

Here a more benevolent construction is put upon the idea of a national mission, a word Bosanquet hesitates to use because it is 'too narrow and too aggressive'.[21] The differences of national character implied in the different missions arise, he thinks, from different experiences and rule out cosmopolitan government for the immediate future. Yet these differences of character are seen, in idealist terms, as reflecting the distinctive *Sittlichkeit*, or social ethics, of each nation, for which Bosanquet provides a historical explanation in terms of the growth of social and political institutions. This is to accord national character a significance it would lack were it to be formed by mere imitation (as we saw Somerset Maugham believing). Bosanquet, therefore, takes issue with this reductive theory as expounded by Gabriel de Tarde and taken up, we might notice, by both McDougall and Barker – the latter mentioning the imitation of great men (like Cromwell for the English!) as a feature of national character formation.

Bosanquet's stress on national experiences, however, finds its best expression in the Austro-Marxist social philosopher Otto Bauer. Clearly he is not an idealist, but he also rejects an economic materialist view of Marxism, seeing individual consciousness as the unit of social explanation. Bauer was writing in the context of nationalist struggles within the Austrian Empire, and he immediately grants significant differences between nations, readily detectable in terms of their national characters, with different ways of thinking and feeling. However, he regards national character not as a causal factor but as marking a type of regularity in acting. Its explanation is not metaphysical, as an expression of *Volksgeist*, or national spirit, nor racial. Rather it reflects the common direction of people's wills, resulting from their shared historical experiences, so that 'a nation can thus be defined as a community of character that grows out of a community of destiny'.[22]

It is easy to see the greater appeal of this account for subject peoples conducting campaigns of national secession or reunification than confident stories of national missions. Its concession of the possibility of changes in character and its emphasis on the role of the will suit it to a liberal application – despite the fact that Bauer opposes his basically cultural criterion of nationhood to Renan's voluntarist one, which unlike Bauer's account, requires a national consciousness. National consciousness, Bauer believes, is a secondary phenomenon which develops only when a national group is brought into contact, possibly confrontational, with other groups. Prior to that its unity is unreflective, a feature other writers, like Barker, attributed to the English, by contrast with the self-conscious nationalism which arises after the French Revolution. In the last analysis, however, Bauer is not, even in our unpejorative sense, a nationalist, believing that each person's national identity can be accommodated by the granting of cultural rights within a multinational state.

The Decline of Character

Up until the First World War most English liberals had been, in our sense, nationalists, conceding nations a right to statehood, on Millian lines, as deriving from a general right of freedom of association, and assuming that autonomy is what groups with distinct national characters would prefer – although practical problems in implementing this liberal programme were acknowledged. After the war, however, disillusion set in as a result of the difficulties of redrawing the map of Europe and the widespread unrest and imposition of authoritarian regimes which this occasioned. The attempt to marry a shared political will to cultural distinctiveness in the way that the theory of national character presupposed, and to draw organisational conclusions from it, began to seem unworkable.

One casualty was the theory of national character itself. Despite eclectic defences like Barker's, it came increasingly under attack in the English-speaking world as a usable criterion of national identity. Writing a year before Barker, the political philosopher R. M. MacIver acknowledges that, while 'there are marked similarities and dissimilarities which distinguish, in certain instances at least, the representative members of one nation from those of another', they are no more marked than the differences between members of what he takes to be sub-national groups, and they are, at best, typical, not criterial of membership of the nation. They are, furthermore, 'too elusive, too subtle, for definition. They are subject accordingly, within the nation, to sentimental simplification and embellishment; and, as between nations, to the most exaggerated and fanciful representation',[23] which changes according to the state of international relations. This last point concerning the malleability of national stereotypes is rather different from one made somewhat later by Harold Laski, who sees national character itself changing quite suddenly in response to circumstances, and he instances the replacement of German 'respect for science and learning . . . by a public veneration for the mystic ravings of a group of gangsters'.[24]

MacIver himself adopts a purely subjectivist account of nationality as 'the sense of community which, under the historical conditions of a particular social epoch, has possessed or still seeks expression through the unity of a state'.[25] He rejects Renan's additional requirement that this arises from recognition of a shared history. MacIver was a strong critic of idealism, but A. D. Lindsay, who remained under its influence adopts a similar criterion of what he terms 'nationality in the political, as distinguished from the personal or cultural sense', though he restricts it to groups already possessing a state: 'It is a sentiment, a readiness to act together, a feeling that the organisation of government of this area is the common job, something that matters to all.'[26] There is more than a hint of the idea of a national mission here, but it is deliberately separated from any idea of a distinctive national culture and its effect on national character, as these are linked by Bosanquet. Lindsay identifies a non-political sense of nationality as consciousness of a common culture, which, by contrast with the position in Western Europe, in Central and Eastern Europe preceded shared political institutions. But, he maintains, these non-political nationalities do not have boundaries appropriate to those of modern states, and they look to the past in deciding upon their political associations, not to 'the common job' that needs to be done in the future. Nationalism on this basis is unacceptably emotional.

Laski goes further than Lindsay. Making no distinction between political and cultural nationality, he declares it to be 'a psychological phenomenon rather than a juridical principle'.[27] He denies that Mill's principle of a national right to statehood is tenable, given that modern states are sovereign bodies pursuing their own interests. Without either social Darwinism or an idealist philosophy of history to draw upon for optimism, Laski sees the consequences of this as ethically deplorable, with adverse effects on personal liberty and international justice. Laski concludes that 'if the nation is entitled to self-government, it is to a self-government limited and defined by the demands of a wider interest.'[28] In this he welcomes the development of an international community, a theme pursued at the same time by MacIver. These philosophers are moving towards a denial of the doctrine of popular sovereignty that seeks an answer to the question 'Who are the people?' by reference to an entity like the nation.

Yet, even as they wrote, this sort of liberal internationalism itself came under attack as the Second World War loomed. The quasi-Marxist political thinker E. H. Carr branded it 'utopianism', and advocated a more clear-sighted 'realism' about power relations and conflicts of interest. He too, though, condemns 'the nineteenth century supposition that nation and state should normally coincide',[29] and its concomitant equation between the principle of self-determination and the principle of nationality. The right of self-determination, he suggests, is a right of individuals to determine their units of political organisation in accordance with their socio-economic interests, so that these units change and attract shifting loyalties as conditions change. Carr would no doubt have regarded talk of national character which seems to stand in the way of this as an ideological construction in the interests of those who benefit from the national status quo.

Talk of national character did not survive the Second World War in educated circles, though it continues to fuel popular fantasies and antagonisms. The reasons for its decline are multifarious. The observed volatility of national characteristics and allegiances, which Laski noted, and their susceptibility to political manipulation, played a part, as did a greater awareness of regional and supranational affiliations. In modern conditions the kind of cultural homogeneity on which talk of national character was predicated could no longer be assured and individual variations of lifestyle were seen to reflect divergent values. This last point reflected a growing liberal belief that the ethical role of the state, even the nation state, was limited to the delivery of procedural justice, allowing maximum scope for the personal choice of values.

Yet a philosophical reaction to this position set in, which corresponded to a resurgence in nationalism following the end of the Cold War. Communitarian thinkers emphasised once more the embeddedness of the individual in a social setting from whose communal practices his or her values supposedly derive. This led to a concern with what came to be known as cultural identity. But, in the language of identity, national character and national identity may be less different than meets the eye, with many of the same questions about what constitutes the former recurring about the latter. National identity may for present purposes be viewed as a species of cultural identity, differentiated from others by the political use to which the notion is put in claiming a right to separate statehood or other forms of autonomy. Other kinds of cultural identity are associated with less ambitious political goals. All, however, share the roles played by national character earlier. First, the appeal to cultural identity aims to secure identification with other members of a putative group. Second, in doing so it aims to justify loyalty and partiality towards them. And third, it seeks to ground a political right. And such grounding is based on the fact that cultural identity is regarded, like national character, as sorting people out into different psychological kinds, and though the naturalistic underpinnings of this, deriving from Herder, have been abandoned, this represents an anti-universalist position very much in his spirit. The politics of cultural identity to which this has given rise sorts people into different kinds, usually, though not invariably, through their supposed possession of different values. Thus cultural pluralism is linked, as in the work of Isaiah Berlin, to value pluralism, and the idea that different nations need different political institutions to pursue what they distinctively value.

Notes

1. David Hume, *An Enquiry Concerning Human Understanding* (many edns), sec. 65.
2. Plato, *Laws* (many edns), Book V.
3. Aristotle, *Politics* (many edns), Book VII.
4. Johann Gottfried von Herder, quoted in R. R. Ergang, *Herder and the Foundations of German Nationalism* (New York, NY: Columbia University Press, 1931), pp. 90–1.

5. Henry Sidgwick, *The Elements of Politics* (London: Macmillan, 1981), p. 11.
6. John Stuart Mill, *Mill on Bentham and Coleridge* (London: Chatto and Windus, 1971), p. 73.
7. Ernest Renan, 'What is a nation?', in A. Zimmern (ed.), *Modern Political Doctrines* (London: Oxford University Press, 1939), p. 203.
8. Ibid. p. 203.
9. Somerset Maugham, *A Writer's Notebook* (London: Heinemann, 1951), p. 142.
10. William McDougall, *An Introduction to Social Psychology* (London: Methuen, 1913), p. 258.
11. Ibid. pp. 298–9.
12. Samuel Smiles, *Character* (London: John Murray, 1939), p. 32.
13. F. H. Bradley, *Ethical Studies* (Oxford: Oxford University Press, 1927), p. 167.
14. Ernest Barker, *National Character and the Factors in its Formation* (London: Methuen, 1927), pp. 2–4.
15. Friedrich Meinecke, *Cosmopolitanism and the National State* (Princeton, NJ: Princeton University Press, 1970).
16. Elie Kedourie, *Nationalism* (London: Hutchinson, 1960), p. 71.
17. Martin Heidegger, 'The self-assertion of the German university', in G. Neske and E. Kettering (eds), *Heidegger and National Socialism* (New York, NY: Paragon House, 1990).
18. T. M. Robinson (ed. and trans.), *Heraclitus: Fragments* (Toronto: University of Toronto Press, 1987), no. 80.
19. Karl Popper, *The Open Society and its Enemies* (London: Routledge and Kegan Paul, 1966), vol. 2, p. 30.
20. Bernard Bosanquet, *The Philosophical Theory of the State and Related Essays* (South Bend, IN: St Augustine's Press, 2001), p. 44.
21. Ibid. p. 283.
22. Otto Bauer, 'The Nation', in G. Balakrishnan (ed.), *Mapping the Nation* (London: Verso, 1996), p. 52.
23. R. M. MacIver, *The Modern State* (London: Oxford University Press, 1926), pp. 124–5.
24. Harold Laski, *Liberty in the Modern State* (Harmondsworth: Penguin, 1937), p. 31.
25. MacIver, *The Modern State*, p. 124.
26. A. D. Lindsay, *The Modern Democratic State* (London: Oxford University Press, 1943), p. 163.
27. Laski, *Liberty*, p. 194.
28. Ibid. p. 199.
29. E. H. Carr, *Conditions of Peace* (London: Macmillan, 1942), p. 62.

3
The Idea of Deep Identity

Herder's Recent Heirs

The broader notion of cultural identity that has emerged from the wreckage of national character has become the common currency of groups in different circumstances, with consequentially different concerns and different political goals. These correspond to some extent to the situations that contributed to the demise of national character. The division of empires after the First World War failed to produce the homogeneous nation states that idealists like Woodrow Wilson had hoped on account of the fact that these states each took in a variety of ethnic groups. The end of colonial empires revealed a similar situation in the newly independent states. Immigration from such states into previously more ethnically homogeneous ones led to it here also. These, and many other factors, created a variety of tensions and dissatisfactions which have been conceptualised in terms of differences of cultural identity. And, in virtue of the complexities of such situations, the political demands defended by reference to such supposed differences are more diverse than the separate statehood, or political accommodation in lieu of it, claimed on the basis of a distinct national character.

Nevertheless, the notion of cultural identity as it is deployed in defending political demands still carries with it the Herderian assumptions of national character. It is worthwhile, then, to briefly look back at some of Herder's own ideas and then forward to those of his contemporary followers who explicitly employ the notions of cultural identity as analytically useful tools rather than merely rhetorical devices. Herder, as we have seen, held two fundamental tenets. The first is that cultures are objectively distinguishable, in the sense that the self-identifications of their members should be based on a recognition of their cultural distinctiveness rather than cultural distinctiveness being the result of their self-identifications. The second is that their individual identities consist in psychological features which are derived in part from their cultural membership. In addition, Herder held two further theses to account for the radical differences which he discerned between cultures. First, he took these differences to consist in part in divergences in values. Second, he believed the different languages of separate cultures to give rise to different world views. While these two theses are separable, both contribute to the notion that members of different cultures will, at the least, have difficulty in understanding and socialising with one another, and consequently that this should be recognised in political arrangements made for them.

Herder's leading twentieth-century follower was Isaiah Berlin, whose work directly influenced philosophical apologists for the politics of cultural identity, like Charles Taylor. It was, however, particularly with regard to national identity that Berlin shaped his specific version of Herderian thought. Thus in endorsing a benign understanding of nationalism, he holds

> that men belong to a particular human group, and that
> the way of life of the group differs from that of others;
> that the characters of the individuals who compose the

group are shaped by, and cannot be understood apart from, those of the group, defined in terms of . . . factors which shape human beings, their purposes and their values.[1]

Among such factors Berlin cites history, customs, beliefs, language, and so on. And he goes on to say that principles are to be followed, not because universally valid, but because

> these values are those of *my* group – for the nationalist, of *my* nation; these thoughts, feelings, this course of action, are good or right, and I shall achieve fulfilment or happiness by identifying myself with them because they are the demands of the particular form of social life into which I have been born.[2]

Such cultural values are, furthermore, incommensurable, in the sense that there is no way of arbitrating between them – a doctrine that Berlin discerns in Herder himself.

It is from this conception of cultural identity that Berlin draws Herderian conclusions concerning the need for recognition of the group of which one is a member, for 'I may feel unfree . . . as a member of an unrecognised or insufficiently respected group',[3] for example my community or nation, since 'my sense of my own moral and social identity [is] intelligible only in terms of the social network of which I am . . . an element.'[4] In the case of nations such recognition will characteristically take the form of allowing self-determination, and Berlin's Zionism is partly based on this general principle, though partly too on the need for a homeland in which Jews can escape persecution. But Berlin's further argument for a Jewish state is that assimilation for the Jews has proved unworkable. This line of thought is presumably generalisable. Given his account of cultural identity, assimilation will always be at least problematic since it is one's original culture which gives one's life its purpose in terms of that culture's values. Thus recognition and accommodation needs to be provided to sustain that identity. Recognition by others is, furthermore and in Hegelian vein, required over and above self-identification for someone to have the identity they have.

Many of these themes from Berlin are taken over by Charles Taylor, to whom the surge of philosophical interest over the last twenty years in the politics of identity is largely attributable. Taylor too takes identity to crucially involve the possession of certain values: 'to have an identity is to know "where you're coming from" when it comes to questions of value, or issues of importance'.[5] Indeed, the connection is so close that he claims of what he calls our strong evaluations, 'shorn of these we would cease to be ourselves'.[6] Taylor thinks, like Berlin, that these values are rooted in a particular culture, and especially a culture constituted by a common language. Here his account is more complex than Herder's or Berlin's, for Taylor sees identity as depending upon self-interpretation, as he puts it. But 'my discovering my own identity doesn't mean that I work it out in isolation, but that I negotiate it through dialogue . . . with others'.[7] Thus 'a self only exists within . . . "webs of interlocution"',[8] that is dialogue with certain interlocuters, and this requires some common language. This interlocution is an aspect of the recognition required for one to have an identity. So for Taylor, as for Herder, identity is a matter of discovery, but it also depends upon the subject seeing herself in a certain way and having her self-conception endorsed by other members of the group. And a further aspect of the way in which she must see herself to have a stable identity is as living her life in terms of a narrative in which her values are, or fail to be, realised.

What is noteworthy about Taylor's complex account is that it aims to build up a picture of cultural identity, which is a collective identity shared by many people, on the basis of metaphysical reflections on what constitutes individual identity. I call them metaphysical since they presuppose something we can think of as a person's *real* identity, behind any of the superficial markers she may mention in saying who she is, and this is a presupposition I shall question later. Here, however, I want to note the various strands in Taylor's account which typify the way many philosophers put together different components of a putative individual identity and, by finding commonalities in them between people, construct their cultural identity on this basis. Thus it is that common values, a common language, a common history and so on, or some mixture of these, are taken to characterise a common cultural identity, and this is supposedly part of an individual's identity because the relevant components are constitutive parts. This picture, derived from the two fundamental tenets of Herder mentioned above, characterises what I term accounts of cultural identity as *deep* identity.

Before investigating this notion further, however, we should pause briefly to consider if Taylor's account is, like Herder's, an objective one, since what he calls self-interpretation is a necessary feature of identity. Let us ask, then, if self-interpretation amounts to self-identification. If it does then there is, I think, a serious problem for Taylor's account, for either it is the objective features which make someone who she is, or who she is is in some way an act of self-creation: it is very hard to see how it could be a mixture of both. But while Taylor speaks of 'my discovering my own identity', which suggests the former, the strong evaluations involved in self-interpretation are not just the values my actions manifest, but those that I endorse as what I choose to live by. On the face of it this looks like a form of self-identification and Taylor does speak of someone's 'self-definition as a Catholic and a Québecois'.[9] Yet the fact that this identification needs to be recognised by others as something other than incoherent or delusional seems to take us back to an objective account where strong evaluations are constitutive not because self-chosen, but because they give an objectively discernible shape to one's life which a mere sequence of divergent or perfunctory valuations would not. This is, I think, an unstable combination, but it is to disentangling the different strands in Taylor's account that I wish to turn, in particular the values, language and narrative which, in his view, together constitute an individual identity, or, when sufficiently shared, a collective cultural one that is a deep identity.

Individual Identity

National character is supposedly, in Bernard Williams's words, 'a deep social classification' in the sense that it can 'explain or underlie a lot of the individual's activities, emotions, reactions and, in general, life.'[10] It is thought of as what I call a *deep* identity – a psychological characteristic of individuals who fall under the classification which explains much of their behaviour, especially those bits of it which distinguish them from those who do not fall under the same classification. Deep identities can be thought of in different ways, depending upon what their explanatory role is taken to be. To illustrate these we need to look at ways of conceiving of individual identity before turning to their analogues in collective cultural identities.

First, then, a conception of individual identity may be deep because it takes a person's identity to explain her behaviour by indicating her motives for action. We can call this an *agentive* (or practical) conception of identity, the idea behind it being that what makes someone the person she is is what provides the wellsprings of her actions. And certainly this is a beguiling and influential picture, not least because it seems to enable us to distinguish behaviour that is really hers from that which is to be explained otherwise than by her agency – as the result of something external to her, in delirium or illness, say, or when she is coerced by another. She, however, seems to retain her identity to the extent to which there is, for the most part, some relatively stable determinant of her behaviour. If there is not then talk of 'multiple identities' and the like might seem to get some foothold.

This conception locates identity, then, in those psychological factors which motivate action. No doubt these are multifarious, but we can conveniently distinguish at least two possible pictures. One, naturalistically inclined, presents these factors as deep-seated drives, both conscious and unconscious, innate or acquired, so that coming to know who one is consists in grasping what these are and coming to terms with them. Another, more rationalistic, views the motivational factors as primarily normative, consisting in the values that a person espouses. These may again be thought of in two ways. The first sees a person's values as her preferences, expressed in her choices as much as in her words: 'finding' one's identity, in this picture, is discovering over time what one's settled preferences are. A second rationalistic picture (like Taylor's) presents a person's values as what she more or less reflectively sets herself to follow and is prepared to offer as good reasons for her acts: her identity consists, then, in those values she identifies with.

The agentive identity conception may, through its concentration upon the springs of action, seem to leave out something crucial to one's identity, namely the way we see the world. The idea of one's identity being constituted by one's thoughts and experiences is, of course, familiar from Descartes, who, asking what he is, concludes that he is a thinking thing. What would individuate such an individual from others of the same sort would be the sort of thoughts they had. But we do not need to regard this identity as that of a mental substance, nor do we need to view the thoughts that characterise it as independent of the world the thinker is in. We can equally view them as giving the thinker's way of thinking about that world, so that her identity consists in the possession of this particular perspective. And this metaphor indicates the way that what we may thus call her *perspectival* identity may be taken to explain features of her thinking and, ultimately, her actions too.

Perspectival identity explains actions by telling us how someone thinks of the world in which she acts, so that her acts are, for the most part, appropriate to that world given what she wants from it. There are, prima facie, two ways of fleshing this idea out, though arguably they merge into each other. We could think of someone as having, in a broad sense, certain theories about the world that explain her acts. She treats one male colleague differently from the others, to use a trivial example, because she believes, from experience or instruction, that men in cowboy boots are not to be trusted. Alternatively, we could think of her as conceptualising the world in a particular way – as classifying men, to return to our example, as predatory or inoffensive, say, which is a scheme that some may apply and others have no use for. The world looks different to her than it does to these others in a way that cannot be captured in their divergent general beliefs, though it too shows in her actions. It is more like, one might suggest, the different styles in which painters may depict the same subject matter, so that the world looks different – quite literally – from their different perspectives.

Either reading of perspectival identity locates what makes a person who she is in whatever psychological characteristics are responsible for her distinctive picture of the world, differing from that of others in content or style. This is not, perhaps, a purely philosophical conception either. We do sometimes want to know, in something like this sense, who someone is, in trying to grasp from what range of thoughts and experiences her current expressions of opinion, say, derive, especially if these opinions are startling or rebarbative. We think of her then as in one way or another seeing the world differently from us and of her individuality as somehow constituted by this difference, whether or not it is something that she thinks of herself as manifesting.

It is in providing a perspective on the world that language is often thought to be an important aspect of a person's deep identity, for language provides a range of concepts, styles, tones and other resources for articulating one's experiences, so that it is through her use of language that a person's particular outlook on the world, and thus her personality, are to a large extent discerned. But language has another, though closely related role, and that is as a medium of communication and association with others. It is what, in Taylor's phrase, establishes one's 'network of interlocution', by providing one with a specific place in it, and this feature is particularly important when we come to consider collective identities based on shared language as what make community possible. Meanwhile, however, we should notice that language is what makes possible the construction of an individual's ongoing narrative of her life.

We turn, then, to the notion of *narrative* identity, which builds upon philosophical accounts of identity in terms of continuity of self-consciousness: what supposedly makes someone the same person over time – gives them their identity in this sense – is the fact that they can remember a series of events in each of which they remember prior members of the series. But narrative identity requires, in addition, that the subject has a reflective grasp of the series as constituting her life, and she does so by incorporating them into a story in which, of course, some events will have a greater significance than others. A person's supposed narrative identity is given by this story of her life, which may allude to events she did not personally witness or remember.

This is not to say that one can make up just any sort of

story about oneself; there are a variety of constraints. 'We are never more (and sometimes less) than the co-authors of our own narratives . . . We enter upon a stage which we did not design and find ourselves part of an action that was not of our making.'[11] The story we tell about ourselves has to cohere, more or less, with the stories other people tell, and each person's story will involve others as characters in it. This is a constraint on what we take the facts to be and how we characterise them. Another constraint is that the story must make sense: I describe myself as following plans, reacting intelligibly to events and so on. Indeed it is this constraint that gives the life narrated the kind of unity that confers identity upon its subject. But what counts as sense here will again be referable to the kinds of story others tell. In this way, an individual's narrative identity depends upon her being 'embedded', in some sense, in a culture of narratives; and the same relation is true of perspectival and agentive identity – for an individual perspective must be part of a collective one, and individual values not utterly divorced from those of others around one. It is for these reasons that collective cultural identities are taken to be presupposed in individual ones.

Here, then, is the opposite, though not incompatible, line of thought from that which sees cultures as constituted by the aggregation of individual characteristics, namely one which sees these characteristics as shaped by culture. Herder seems to have taken the former line of thought to give an explanation of why shared cultures are as they are, for they come about as a result of individuals reacting in the same way to the same environments into which they are thrown; though, in accordance with the latter line, their shared language creates a common sensibility. It is the latter line, rather than the former with its naturalistic overtones, that later thinkers have tended to rely upon, seeing individual cultural characteristics as the internalisation of cultural norms and frameworks of thought. But then the assumption is that there are shared cultures providing such resources internalised by their members in such a way as to yield the sorts of deep psychological features of individuals which we have looked at, and to yield them as shared features; for it is this that makes the cultures shared. And then these cultures are taken to be one and the same as what pass as the cultures of groups making political claims, since, after all, it is on the basis of such supposedly deep-going common characteristics that the claims are lodged.

It is these last two assumptions which we shall be investigating. For we do not need to deny that there are deep-going features of individual psychology of the sort we have looked at, nor that these derive, in some way, from cultural norms and frameworks, though whether they constitute individual identities in any normal sense is questionable. But do these cultural resources constitute individuatable cultures? And are the cultural groups making political claims formed from the members of such cultures?

Conceptions of Culture

The accounts of culture that have been offered by political theorists are intended to mirror their metaphysical accounts of individual identity, since it is commonalities in one or more of the constituents of this that supposedly form people into a group with a shared culture. Let us start, then, with the idea of cultures being constituted, at least partly, by shared values. Cultural identity is, indeed, often thought of in terms of subscription to a distinctive set of values. A topical example is the supposedly distinct identity of Muslims from that of the western Europeans and Americans among whom they dwell or from whom, wherever they dwell, they feel threatened by forces of cultural imperialism. An example of a value now largely absent from Western culture but dominant in Islam is purity. The importance and significance of purity in Islam is expressed in ritual ablutions before prayers, bathing after sexual intercourse, the avoidance of alcohol, and numerous other cultural practices. In the absence of such practices it has, in the contemporary West, little resonance as a value in most people's lives. Are there, then, good reasons for recognising that there are distinct cultural identities here, conceived in terms of divergent values, where to speak of an identity is to speak of a certain sort of person, not just of someone who shares practices and associations with certain others?

The idea here will be that, to the extent to which people share a culture so conceived, members will draw upon the same sort of reasons for their actions – reasons which appeal to the same values, aspirations, attachments and so on. As just noted, it is this conception of culture which we have already seen at work in the notion of distinct national characters which precedes that of cultural identities, and in which character is regarded as constituted by adherence to a range of values and the like. Thus, in contrasting English national character adversely with that of the Germans in the nineteenth century, Heinrich von Treitschke wrote:

> The English possess a commercial spirit, a love of money which has killed every sentiment of honour . . . In England all notions of honour and class prejudices vanish before the power of money, whereas the German nobility has remained poor but chivalrous.[12]

Here, a certain kind of culture is comprehensively characterised and condemned in terms of what does and does not motivate its members, and what then gives them the national character and cultural identity they have.

The English would not, of course, have described their own culture in quite these terms. Rather they would have viewed their motivations as displaying enterprise and progressiveness, by contrast with those of their German contemporaries. The justification for terming culture, conceived in the way we are now thinking of it, as *value culture* is that, if it is to furnish its members with reasons to act, then these must be considerations which they can recognise as reasons because they value what their acts should achieve. What distinguish value cultures so understood will be not only the different ranges and priorities of values they pursue but their different ideals, distinctive collective projects and specific shared affections and repugnances. All these are taken to be internalised by those who grow up within or are otherwise acculturated into a certain cultural framework, and it is this internalisation which supposedly yields a deep identity, whether or not it is recognised as such by those who possess it. It is, furthermore, assumed that what is thus shared between members of the culture constitutes the deepest wellsprings of action, for what could go deeper than motivations acquired in the course of acquiring a culture?

Yet even if some such account of culture is accepted we should notice straightaway that there is, as yet, no reason to think it yields the sort of cultural identities for which political claims are typically made. There is no reason, that is to say, to simply assume that the lines it draws around cultures in terms of the values they inculcate – if lines there are to be drawn at all – follow the demarcation of supposedly politically significant cultural identities. To take the case of national cultures, it is noteworthy that von Treitschke speaks only of the upper classes in nineteenth century England and Germany. Neither the love of money nor the defence of honour were relevant motivations for their respective working classes, whose cultural frameworks would in fact have been quite different from those of their betters, however much they were encouraged to identify with them. And similar considerations apply quite generally.

Yet it is not only insofar as certain values go deep with some members of a group and not with others that such values are inapt to characterise what is normally thought of as a specific cultural or national identity. Insofar as values like purity are shared among Muslims, for example, there is no reason to suppose that they characterise anything deep going in their psychological make-up. The value of purity is manifest in Muslim practices of ablution and purification, so that it is participation in these that lead to ascription of the value. We do not need to think of these practices as somehow motivated by inner states that involve this valuation, by, for instance, feelings of dirtiness prior to the ritual. Similarly with putatively English values of fair play, reserve and so on: these are manifest in queuing rather than jostling for drinks, shaking hands rather than embracing and so forth. Nothing inner is needed to explain these habitual patterns of behaviour. Indeed, insofar as the relevant values do explain them they do so only by fitting them into a pattern, not by attributing specific motives. Individual motives may, in fact, differ widely, including the desire to conform to what one inwardly despises. As the anthropologist Anthony Cohen puts it in speaking of rituals, 'common forms do not generate common meanings'.[13] But lip service like this may well suffice for group membership.

Furthermore, however, it is quite unclear that subscription to English values, in the sort of sense we have given this notion, requires one to be motivated by them at all. And nor need this be due to weakness of will recognised as such by its victims. Emotional, boastful people with no fondness for animals abound among the English, as anywhere else, and they may perceive no incongruity between their own behaviour and their protestations of Englishness; for it is quite possible to value certain traits in others, with whom one professes an affinity of valuation, yet not be actuated by them oneself. Nor, though they may be the object of occasional mild disapproval, need such people be pressured to change their behaviour, perhaps because it is not even obvious that they are a minority.

The vagueness of a value criterion for delimiting a cultural identity is one political reason why a language criterion is often preferred. But there are also philosophical reasons for favouring an account of cultures as held together by shared meanings, and, in particular, by the shared meanings provided by a common language – to think of them, as we shall say, as *language cultures*. Many cultural identities are supposedly founded on a shared language. Pan-Arab nationalism, for example, was based on the belief in a common Arab identity deriving from the speaking of a single Arabic language. Nor is this feature lost in contemporary pan-Islamic fundamentalism, for though many Muslims do not speak Arabic as their native tongue it is the language of their holy book, the Koran, because so revealed by God to Mohammed, and it is this that gives Arabic its particular prestige. As the divine language it provides those who possess it with a privileged understanding – an understanding lost, according to tradition, in translation; for other languages are allegedly less precise and rich than Arabic. Thus it is the Arabic language which endows Arabs with wisdom and other moral qualities. It is crucial, then, that Arabic is spoken correctly and corrupt speech, possibly resulting from foreign importations, threatens inauthenticity and the loss of identity.

To think of cultures as constituted by language may be thought to capture what the perspectives of their members have in common. For, though these perspectives will differ in respect of the individual opinions or attitudes that they involve, what they share, it may be argued, is the framework of linguistic and other cultural signifiers which make it possible to formulate and express such beliefs about, and relations to, the world. There is a sense, in this conception, in which those who share a language, broadly understood, share a world – a world distinct from that of those with a different language, with its different range of meanings and associations. Cultural identity, on this view of culture, is therefore that form of perspectival identity which is shared by members of the culture.

What has here been generalised to members of a culture has been the second version of individual perspectival identity which I distinguished earlier. The first, we may recall, involved a set of general beliefs about the world rather than, in the second, a way of conceptualising it – which is clearly what a language provides one with. There may sometimes be reasons for attributing shared general beliefs to members of a culture, but if they share a language then at least they have a way of conceptualising the world in common.

Language culture may again seem to furnish a very deep identity, and for a similar sort of reason for which value culture identity did, namely that it is an identity acquired in acculturation that makes individual beliefs and attitudes possible at all. What the identity supposedly provides is a structure within which these relations to the world can be formulated and expressed and which is thus more basic than an individual's particular perspective with its contingent and changeable contexts. Indeed a language culture identity can seem more basic than a value culture one precisely because a change of values, from conversion to a religion say, may appear to be possible only within the persisting framework of meanings shared between believers and unbelievers.

Yet attention to this kind of case exemplifies the implausibility of delimiting cultural identities so conceived along the lines of spoken languages, as many nationalists, for example, would do. There are, on the one hand, enormous differences in the ranges of meanings available to different speakers of the same language, dependent upon just such facts as whether they have been inducted into its use in religious contexts or, more generally, what sorts of literary productions or vernacular practices they are at home with. And, on the other hand, similarities in respect of such familiarities cut across the boundaries of spoken languages.

There are, furthermore, many languages, like English, that are spoken by members of what would be thought of as distinct cultural groups. Thus, despite William Butler Yeats's identification with Ireland, he wrote that 'I owe my soul . . . to the English language in which I think, speak and write; that everything I love has come to me through English.'[14] English was a deep-going aspect of his individual identity, but it was not part of what collected together the Irish, many of whom still spoke Gaelic. As with value culture, language culture does not seem to offer the kind of criterion that those who make political claims on the basis of it typically take it to provide, if it is taken to yield a shared perspective.

We might, however, think of a language culture in terms of a specific range of language speakers. 'I am a self,' writes Taylor, 'only in relation to certain interlocuters', and he goes on to say that 'the full definition of someone's identity thus usually involves . . . some reference to a defining community',[15] and exemplifies this as 'Québecois'. Thus he is thinking of membership of a particular community as part of a person's identity. According to Karl Deutsch, 'Insofar as a common culture facilitates communication, it forms a *community*',[16] and his notion of community here is that of a collection of people related by their capacity to communicate. Indeed he regards 'culture' and 'community' as names of the same thing, so that cultural identity consists in membership of such a community. Let us leave to one side here our earlier criticism of conflating culture and community, and note that Deutsch regards 'the channels of culture'[17] as transmitting knowledge, values, customs and so on. But it is not commonality in any of these that constitutes cultural identity: it is the scope of communicating them, and this is usually, though not always, determined by a common language.

'Peoples,' writes Deutsch, 'are held together "from within" by this communicative efficiency',[18] so it would seem that he regards their identity so construed as explanatory of this further fact about their relationships. Deutsch is sensitive to the criticism that there may be greater communicative complementarity between people who would ordinarily be thought to come from different cultures, and a lack of it within the same one. In respect of the former, as exemplified by vocational groups, say, he suggests that this is 'limited to a relatively narrow segment of their total range of activities',[19] in respect of the latter, that there really may be, in Disraeli's phrase, 'two nations' if communication between social classes, for instance, breaks down. Yet he nowhere provides a clear criterion of what counts as adequate communicative complementarity to constitute a single culture, and hence make possible a single community. And this seems to be a general problem in regarding the possibility of association mediated by a common language as at least partly constituting cultural identity.

Even if we could overcome this problem, however, we encounter another difficulty. For it is not at all clear that the communicative identity in question could really explain behaviour in the manner of a deep identity. What it explains – various ways of relating to others – is not accounted for by it in terms of the agents' valuing them, for instance, but only as the means of relating she shares with those to whom she relates. But this looks like an explanation which simply fits her behaviour into an expected pattern, rather than as arising from any psychological state. Doubtless the agent must in some way internalise the required modes of behaviour, but there is so far no reason to ascribe psychological correlates to such an internalisation – any more than we would, say, to a disposition to pronounce words in one accent rather than another.

So far we have looked at cultures in synchronic terms – at what they are like at a given time. But cultures can also be viewed diachronically, as having a history and development. Thus, just as membership of a nation is sometimes thought of as being part of a national story, cultural identity more generally can be conceived as membership of a continuing group with its own distinct history and traditions, and with, in some sense, the potential for a future. This could equally be a small village community, say, as a nation. I shall term this a *chronicle culture*, since in some way or another the relevant culture is taken to be individuated by reference to a story about itself unfolding over time. Membership of such a culture thus involves participation in this story. We can see at once, then, that the narrative identities of individuals can be viewed as contributing to a chronicle culture, whether in a large way for a few or a small one for many. Their cultural identity is, on this conception, construed as what their narrative identities have in common, namely, possession of the shared structure which the culture's chronicle supposedly provides. This is, then, a deep identity to the extent to which that chronicle plays a part in the way the individual constructs a narrative for her individual life and sees her actions, aspirations, and experiences in terms of it.

Some putative cultural identities do seem rooted in the past, the cultures to which they refer picked out by a distinctive history. The identity claimed by Ulster Protestants is of this sort. They see themselves as separated from their Catholic countrymen not just by religion, but by a history in which their religion has been and continues to be defended against real or supposed threats. Their individual narratives are woven into this story, if only through attendance at celebrations of the 'Glorious Twelfth' and so forth. A precondition for their claimed cultural identity is, then, that their culture has an identity separate from that of any overarching Irish one. If this is to be viewed in terms of a separate history then it is clearly constructed, in the sense that it is this particular story that the Ulster Protestants tell about themselves and not another which they share with Catholics as inhabitants of the same island with many common experiences. It is undoubtedly the case that this particular story is told and, in that sense, the culture exists.

There is, however, a great deal of room for variation here and that is a prima facie drawback of this criterion of cultural identity. Is it plausible to suppose that people do structure their individual narratives in terms of a common chronicle, a national one for example, in anything other than the banal way that people who have been involved in the same events will need to mention them in recounting their lives? This falls short of what is required since these events need not then be thought of as part of the shared history of a group, rather as merely individual afflictions or blessings. And if members of the culture do not so regard them, is it obvious that they should? It just is not clear why the chronicle of one group rather than another – one's nation, for example, rather than one's village – should be adopted as the structure for an individual's narrative; or, indeed, why the chronicle of any group at all should be. And even if it is, it is not clear that this aspect of identity need have the kind of depth such a structure is meant to provide. That this is part of one's narrative might seemingly explain little or nothing about one's behaviour in the way that nationalists, for example, think that being part of one's nation's history should do. It seems impossible to move from the supposed depth of an individual narrative in terms of the way it structures a life to a similarly deep cultural one.

It might be objected here that the way culture can contribute to an individual's narrative and thus furnish her with a cultural identity has been too narrowly drawn if it is the culture's history – its chronicle – which has to be involved. An apparently different way of making the connection between culture and narrative identity is by seeing one's culture as providing its members with what we might call scripts: narratives that people can use in shaping their projects and in telling their life stories.[20] It is as a character in such a script that one lives one's life and, insofar as such a character is distinctive of a certain culture, one lives it as a member of this culture. There is, however, an ambiguity here between the kinds of life a culture makes possible (or impossible) and the kinds of story it allows one sensibly to tell about a life. Only the former sets cultural limits on one's own narrative since the latter will allow for stories about members of other cultures as well as one's own. Yet only the latter is a narrative resource.

Identity as a Political Expedient

I have tried to sketch different ways of regarding cultural identity which parallel the different accounts of individual identity looked at previously. They are what I called deep conceptions of cultural identity precisely because they take the features which the accounts of individual identity mention to be deep-going aspects of individual psychology, which explain in various ways important facets of behaviour, and then suppose that commonalities in these features can be found which yield deep cultural identities. What I have been suggesting is that insofar as such features are deep they cannot be detected across a range of individuals in such a way as to map out the sorts of things taken to be shared cultural identities. And, conversely, insofar as common features of such identities are discernible they are not, or do not need to be, deep aspects of individual psychology. No doubt these claims require further justification and some will be provided later.

What I shall not attempt to do, however, is to analyse in detail the various philosophical accounts of supposedly deep cultural identities that have been offered, since I take these accounts to be misguided at the outset. This is because they aim to provide metaphysical stories about shared cultural identities in which various components are combined to produce what many authors speak of in such terms as 'a full definition of a person's identity'.[21] I confess to being mystified by such phrases. For the notion that individuals each have a complex identity with various cultural components, a subset of which can be detected across a range of them as their 'cultural identity', seems to me purely metaphysical in that it prescinds from the political application of that term to give it a greater significance than merely speaking of co-religionists, fellow speakers of a language and so forth would have.

In fact, however, the notion of cultural identity is 'inescapably political'.[22] To invoke it is to set out upon a general ethical justification of various sorts of special treatment for putative cultural groups. And, as I indicated earlier, the strategy here is to take what is supposedly owed to people in virtue of their individual identities and transfer the obligation to the way they should be treated as members of a group in virtue of their supposedly shared cultural identity. Since it is only to the extent to which some psychological feature of a person's identity goes deep with her that there is taken to be a duty to recognise it in one's dealings with her, so a cultural identity must be theorised as something deep for the ethical demand to carry over to it. Religious beliefs are the paradigm of this. But while in the individual case one might be careful not to give offence to someone one knows to be, say, a devout Catholic, that anything comparable is owed to a group, most of whom may be only nominally so, is at least questionable. It is the easy assumption of it being a feature of their deep identity that facilitates this transition and many like it.

Depending upon the way that cultural identity is theorised a wide variety of arguments have been assembled to show that it is important for individuals, in the sense that their psychological functioning is somehow impaired if it is in a number of different ways interfered with or not taken account of in their treatment by others. All of these ways are viewed as cases of non-recognition, the result of which is taken to be significant detriment to individuals as psychologically well-functioning systems. Herderian organic analogies hover in the background here, of, for example, plants being trained in ways that go against their nature. A classic example is Will Kymlicka's conception of culture, construed principally in terms of a group's language and history, providing a 'context of choice',[23] as he puts it, for its members. It provides, that is to say, the range of options for their actions, so that if this is somehow unsettled by sudden exposure to other norms or by proscription of their own then the result is supposedly confusion or anomie. Kymlicka exemplifies the supposed process by reference to the situation of American Indians, but this a priori explanation of their plight stands in the way of detailed empirical explanation, as with many other such cases.

It is, in fact, far from clear what the importance of a cultural identity for individuals is meant to consist in. We are to suppose that everyone has an identity with the psychological features some of which, if and when common to others, constitute a cultural identity. Generally, then, we can assume that having such an individual identity is sufficient for one to function properly whether or not this commonality is detectable. A thoroughly cosmopolitan identity would be as good as any other. Sudden shocks to any system or demands that it function in adverse conditions may be problematic, but so far there is no reason to think that identity should not be complicated or adaptable. Thus the often used appeal to the need for a 'secure identity' as what recognition provides surely should not be taken to be a demand for an unchanging one – though one suspects it often is. Rather it should charitably be construed as invoking the desirability of a solid and stable identity which, while open to internal change, is not prone to erratic shifts which could be regarded as psychologically aberrant in the fairly clear sense of making coherent explanation of behaviour impossible.

But why should we suppose that a *cultural* identity is

important for people in preventing this? If one has an identity with the right structure anyway, why should it matter whether or not some of its components are shared in the delimited way that supposedly constitutes a cultural identity? It is in this connection that one sometimes comes across references to the *need* for a cultural identity. Now, distinguishing this from the different idea that there is a need to identify oneself with some culture, which itself seems highly questionable, we have here the notion that it is important for oneself that some of the components of one's identity are shared with fellow members of a culture. It is impossible to speculate why this should be so in the abstract. We need to look at the different postulated components of identity. One's language, we may notice at once, is necessarily shared with others. One's values are, severally if not collectively, also shared, since one could not understand what it would be to make a totally idiosyncratic evaluation of something. And one's individual narrative fits into *some* wider one. So what is at issue is whether the sharing involved in such cases needs to be with members of what is regarded as a cultural group rather than with those of some broader or narrower collection of people; and I cannot see that it does so far as psychological functioning is concerned. Perhaps membership of a well-defined cultural group might make one's values more clear cut or one's narrative tidier, and perhaps this might make individuals' identities more stable. But equally it might make them less flexible and responsive, and so in this respect less well functioning.

Philosophers typically construct a unitary notion of cultural identity, sometimes, as with Taylor, a highly complex one combining several components. One driver for this, not usually explicitly acknowledged, is a desire to find what is most important for people psychologically. Thus we can view Kymlicka's deliberate exclusion of values from his account of a culture, in favour of a language providing a context of choice, as an attempt to locate something more basic than values, which makes values, and indeed even conflicting values within the group, possible. There is perhaps an assumption here that what constitutes people's true or dominant cultural identity is that which is most important for them. On that basis identities based on religion, say, would be less fundamental than language-based ones. But, appealing as such suggestions might be, there is no prospect of such a criterion having any political purchase.

The fact is that which account of cultural identity is chosen by groups making political claims is determined by which delimits the group in the appropriate way. Thus while in the break-up of empires after the First World War the majority Serbo-Croat language served to fashion a separate Yugoslav state, it has been Catholicism versus Orthodoxy that has been partly responsible for its division. There just are no agreed criteria on what constitutes a national identity, nor more generally a cultural one. And, though for consistency groups should only recognise claims which are based on the same criteria as their own, fortunately for international and domestic peace philosophical disagreements over what constitutes cultural identity do not always spill over into political disputes.

There are, of course, conflicts, often violent ones, stemming from clashing criteria over, for instance, claims to statehood. The attempt to hold Yugoslavia together against Croat secession is one example; opposition to the separation of the Six Counties from the rest of Ireland is another. In these circumstances what is characteristically appealed to is not which identity is important *for* people, but which is important *to* them, or which *ought* to be important to them. Now, whereas there should be some general answer to the question which identity is more important for people, if the kind of metaphysical accounts we have been looking at are correct, it is clear that there is no universal answer to the question which is more important to them, in the sense of which they attach greater importance to. In some cases it may be to religion that they attach most importance in allying themselves with some and distinguishing themselves from others for some political purpose. In other cases it may be other features, but in none is there any reason to think that the features to which people attach significance are those that explain major swathes of behaviour in the way that marks a supposed deep identity. Religion in Northern Ireland, for example, is still accorded great significance despite a falling off of observance and a considerable coincidence in moral values between Catholics and Protestants, both groups tending to be much less liberal on social issues that the rest of the UK. There are, then, few differences in behaviour in general aside from mutual avoidance or antagonism.

If we consider the tactics of identity-group activists, we may notice that they seek to make a certain identity important to its prospective members so that they rally to the cause. They may sometimes do so by trying to demonstrate that it is already important for them, when their consequent self-identification will have the character of a discovery. If the foregoing is correct then this will seldom be more than a rhetorical device. Alternatively, though, it may be contended that the identity in question *ought* to be important to people on ethical grounds. That someone should attach particular significance to his being a Muslim, for example, might be urged on the grounds of its superior morality. That an Ulster Protestant should overlook his religious differences and embrace a common Irishness might be canvassed on the grounds that shared occupancy of a place generates an entitlement to a common allegiance. Many very different examples could be adduced, each advocating attachment to a specific identity as ethically required or desirable. But again it is hard to see what general ethical arguments might be provided, and thus for each there are likely to be ethical counter-arguments for different attachments, so that no particular cultural component of identity seems ethically privileged.

A brave attempt to overcome this difficulty has been made by Satya Mohanty[24] who maintains that the identity to which one ought to adhere is that which makes best sense of the world from one's own standpoint in terms of the narrative and other theoretical resources which it offers. This is in a certain sense one's true identity because it is based on genuine knowledge, rather than mystification. Attractive as the suggestion is, however, it fails to offer one a usable criterion since what *seems* to make the best sense will inevitably be tainted by one's wish to make an identification which is pleasurable or comforting rather than, as may be the case with truth seeking, painful or disturbing; and these tendencies will be exploited by those who have an ideological interest in one's adopting a specific identity. Nor is it clear why a narrative or perspectival identity that makes sense of things for one should be prioritised over an agentive identity which provides values to live by. There seems to be no sound ethical grounding for any particular sort of cultural identity. What cultural content an identity has – values, language, history or whatever – is determined by purely political considerations and these are those that weigh with prospective group members.

Notes

1. Isaiah Berlin, *Against the Current* (Princeton, NJ: Princeton University Press, 1979), p. 341.
2. Ibid. p. 143.
3. Isaiah Berlin, *Four Essays on Liberty* (Oxford: Oxford University Press, 1969), p. 157.
4. Ibid. p. 155.
5. Charles Taylor, 'The dialogical self', in J. Bohman, D. Hiley and R. Shusterman (eds), *The Interpretive Turn* (Ithaca, NY: Cornell University Press, 1991), pp. 305–6.

6. Charles Taylor, *Philosophical Papers I* (Cambridge: Cambridge University Press, 1985), p. 34.

7. Charles Taylor, *Philosophical Arguments* (Cambridge, MA: Harvard University Press, 1995), p. 231.

8. Charles Taylor, *Sources of the Self* (Cambridge, MA: Harvard University Press, 1989), p. 36.

9. Charles Taylor, *Multiculturalism and the Politics of Recognition* (Princeton, NJ: Princeton University Press, 1992), p. 36.

10. Bernard Williams, 'Identity and identities', in H. Harris (ed.), *Identity* (Oxford: Clarendon Press, 1995), p. 9.

11. Alastair MacIntyre, *After Virtue* (London: Duckworth, 1985), p. 213.

12. Heinrich von Treitschke, quoted in L. Greenfeld, *Nationalism* (Cambridge, MA: Harvard University Press, 1992), pp. 377–8.

13. Anthony Cohen, *Self Consciousness* (London: Routledge, 1994), p. 20.

14. William Butler Yeats, quoted in R. F. Foster, *Paddy and Mr Punch* (London: Allen and Unwin, 1993), pp. 303–5.

15. Taylor, *Sources of the Self*, p. 36.

16. Karl Deutsch, 'Peoples, nations and communication', in D. Potter and P. Sarre (eds), *Dimensions of Society* (London: Hodder and Stoughton, 1974), p. 129.

17. Ibid. p. 130.

18. Ibid. p. 138.

19. Ibid. p. 138.

20. Antony Appiah, *The Ethics of Identity* (Princeton, NJ: Princeton University Press, 2005), p. 22.

21. Matthew Festenstein, *Negotiating Diversity* (Cambridge: Polity, 2005), p. 24.

22. Chandran Kukathas, *The Liberal Archipelago* (Oxford: Oxford University Press, 2003), p. 9.

23. Will Kymlicka, *Liberalism, Community and Culture* (Oxford: Oxford University Press, 1989), p. 166.

24. Satya Mohanty, 'The epistemic status of cultural identity', in P. M. C. Moya and M. R. Hames-Garcia (eds), *Reclaiming Identity* (Berkeley, CA: University of California Press, 2000).

4
Types of Identity

Crooked Timber and Bent Twigs

The revival of interest in Herder and his doctrine of the political importance of cultural diversity is in large part due to Isaiah Berlin. But, as David Miller has observed,[1] Berlin has two quite different accounts of the political expression of such diversity in movements like nationalism. On the one hand he associates the Herderian doctrine with Kant's remark that 'Out of the crooked timber of humanity no straight thing was ever made',[2] and regards the desire for separate treatment as a natural consequence of these irregularities across humankind. Berlin glosses Herder approvingly:

> There is a plurality of incommensurable cultures. To belong to a given community, to be connected with its members by indissoluble and impalpable ties of common language, historical memory, habit, tradition and feeling is a basic human need no less natural than that for food or drink or security or procreation. One nation can understand and sympathise with the institutions of another only because it knows how much it means to itself. Cosmopolitanism is the shedding of all that makes one most human, most oneself.[3]

Nationalism, on this crooked timber account, is the natural outcome of this diversity.

On the other hand, Berlin also attributes nationalism to people being 'confined and contracted in their universe; they were like Schiller's bent twig, which always jumped back and hit its bender',[4] so that, on this contrasting story, political expressions of identity stem from external and contingent constraints. Miller himself would like to square these two stories. While rejecting Herder's views of national identity as primordial, he nonetheless sympathises with the importance that Herder ascribes to it as one aspect of personal identity, with consequent claims to national self-determination. We may reasonably suppose that analogous considerations hold for cultural identities generally. But if, as I should like to suggest, we reject the crooked timber standpoint wholesale then the bent twig story begins to look attractive as a general explanation of identity politics.

Rejecting the crooked timber picture, we should notice, involves abandoning the idea of peoples differentiated from each other by their separate cultures in ways that are objective and pre-political. It is a thesis, not about the existence of cultural difference, but about the significance of such differences in delimiting groups of people in ways that have consequential political implications; for example, implications for separate statehood in the case of supposedly national cultures. Instead, to adopt the bent twig story is to insist that all such divisions into separate cultural groups have an external explanation, in the sense that they are the result of specific sorts of material and political circumstances. And more than this, it is to claim that the shape of such groups, the way they are delimited from others, depends upon these circumstances. What sort of shape they have, that is to say, depends upon what sort of circumstances they find themselves in. This is the aspect of the bent twig story I intend to build upon, for, though in Berlin's version it is undeveloped and somewhat circumscribed, it is, I believe, capable of providing us with a useful taxonomy of cultural, including national, identities.

There are, I think, three general aspects to Berlin's bent twig story that are worth noticing. First, a group of people are placed in a similar situation by the actions and positions of others, whether deliberate or unintentional. Second, their reactions are entirely understandable. Third, these are, however, sometimes potentially dangerous, especially to those responsible for the position the group is placed in. Berlin's own example is the rise of German nationalism which he imputes to the humiliation Germans experienced because regarded as culturally inferior to the French and other European nations. It is not clear that he himself wishes to move much beyond this kind of case, but it is evident that the sort of wind that bent this twig is not the only kind. Not all nationalism, or other species of cultural identarianism, is a reaction to being in this sort of position. The peripheral nationalism of the Northern League in Italy, for example, represents something like the reverse of this situation, with northerners regarding themselves as justifiably contemptuous of their southern compatriots, not vice versa. Nor is there any reason to think that, in the appropriate circumstances, this sort of nationalism would be any less dangerous than the kind of which Berlin writes. In either case, political ambitions that are baulked can, if accompanied by discordant identities, seek their realisation in precipitate and intemperate violence.

The aim, then, is to distinguish different kinds of political circumstance which have the general features sketched above in order to classify the types of cultural and national identities that flow from them. The first thing to notice about the project is that it is entirely different from any attempt to classify these sorts of identity in terms of differences in the *content* of the cultures involved. It is notorious, as Renan noted, that national identities, for example, cannot be uniformly picked out in terms of differences of language or religion, say. Some employ the one to mark relevant differences, some the other, and many further markers are employed. We may then classify these identities in terms of such diverse markers. The bent twig typology, however, cuts right across this, classifying the twig shapes in terms of the sort of wind that bends them, so to speak, not in terms of the sort of tree on which they grow.

The bent twig typology is again different from, though more clearly connected with, one in terms of the political *aims* of cultural identity groups. National identity, I have argued, consists in membership of a group which claims a right to independent statehood for the group or has some closely analogous claim. This can be expressed in a variety of aspirations depending upon the group's situation. One typology[5] distinguishes nationalisms which aim to *incorporate* people into a state, to *unify* people into a single political body, or to *secede* from an existing state structure. In each case, the aims can be realised by drawing on a variety of cultural features, depending upon which best suits the situation. Secession, for instance, can be based on differences of religion or of language, whichever best identifies the would-be secessionists and which can be used in an argument for separate statehood. Similar considerations apply to incorporation and unification: whatever cultural affinities best justify membership of an existing state or justify shared statehood, respectively, being appealed to.

A bent twig typology, however, classifies identities in terms not of the *aims* of an identity group but of the *circumstances* in which people are placed that form them into a group, whose members' reactions may involve a variety of aims. But the way we characterise these circumstances is important. We could think of them as purely external, with a view to arriving at sociological generalisations about kinds of identity movement and the way they depend on empirically observable social and political situations. But this is not how Berlin develops his bent twig account; for on this it is the external circumstances *as experienced by the people exposed to them* that are responsible for their assertion of an identity. It is, for example, being placed in a situation felt as humiliating that leads the Germans to see themselves as having a certain sort of shared identity, and, as a result of this, to seek national unification. Thus the sort of explanation of identity provided by mentioning people's circumstances is not strictly an empirical one, but one that makes their identitarian reactions understandable. It is, therefore, along these lines that we will look for a bent twig typology of identities.

Identity as Standing

In adopting this approach, what I hope to persuade you of is that there is no unitary notion of cultural, including national, identity: that the different types of identification we shall discern as responses to different sorts of circumstance go by the same name only because they are used in similar ways politically, not because they express some deep feature that all those who claim a cultural identity possess. And I shall try to show this by suggesting what having each of the types of identity consists in. The obvious way to pursue this idea, then, is to ask what those who assert one identity might be concerned about lacking or losing, such that having the identity supplies this lack or loss. If the lacks or losses are different then there is no reason to think that what supplies them will be the same. I want, then, to suggest that the way external circumstances which normally give rise to the assertion of identity are experienced is precisely as revealing a lack or threatening a loss. This is a presupposition of the bent twig model, with its assumption that without what is felt as adverse interference the twig would be straight and then without the political energy for a reaction.

Having an identity and asserting one are intimately linked here, so that it is not just the assertion that circumstances produce, but the possession of a certain type of identity too. This is also a presumption of our model, though this may seen an implausible one when it is the loss of identity that is feared, for this seems to presuppose its prior existence. But notice that if what is feared is the loss of identity, identity is part of the intentional object of fear, so that it need not then exist, any more than a believer's fear that his god will desert him presupposes the existence of that god. Arguably, then, possible loss of identity is just one way in which the insecurity felt in certain circumstances is conceptualised, so that the identification made in response is correspondingly thought of as the reassertion of an identity, whether or not there is any sense in which it did previously exist in that form.

How, then, can we start to classify the winds that bend the twigs of national and analogous cultural identities? Let us begin by thinking of what sorts of insecurity, shared between members of some groups who find themselves treated similarly by others, might lead them to identify with each other in a view of themselves that enables them to counter that insecurity. We have already noticed, in Berlin's own example, a case of this, namely insecurity over whether a people has dignity. They feel themselves undervalued by others and in consequence form a view of themselves as possessing properties which confer self-worth. This constitutes their identity in these circumstances. It is, one might say, identity as *standing*. To have such an identity is to be somebody rather than, as the phrase goes, a nobody. It is to have a place, or at least to claim a place, among the members of one's own and other cultural groups. For the materials with which standing is constructed are cultural ones – characteristically some range of values supposedly applying to members of the group which they can all sign up to.

In the German case these values involved a specific conception of honour, though, as I indicated, some form of honour or dignity is involved in all identities of this type, for in these sorts of case 'if honour is lost, identity is annihilated'.[6] But in different cultures honour has a different content. Among the Germans it pervasively involved military virtues of prowess, valour and loyalty, leading Heinrich von Treitschke to compare them with the English, to the latter's disadvantage:

> In England all notions of honour . . . vanish before the power of money, whereas the German nobility has remained poor but chivalrous. That last indispensable bulwark against the brutalisation of society – the duel – has gone out of fashion in England.[7]

It is, of course, national *characters* that are being compared here. For one employment of the notion of national character is precisely to capture the idea of identity as standing which I have just sketched. The role of character, in this modulation of the notion, is to provide people with traits they can think of themselves as possessing and, in virtue of possessing them, feel pride in themselves, experience the self-worth of which the contempt of others threatened to deprive them. This is the shape of the twig bent by this particular kind of wind.

It is not only what we may most naturally think of as national character which instantiates identity as standing. The kind of Muslim identity fostered by Islamic fundamentalists is, in many respects, another example. It can be seen as the product of a reaction to the Westernising forces of European imperialism, starting with Napoleon's invasion of Egypt, continuing through the dissolution of the Ottoman Empire into mandated territories, and persisting to this day. The reaction to Western attitudes disparaging of Muslim society has been, of course, the assertion of an identity whose bearers can take pride in traditional cultural traits conspicuously absent in the West. For there, as the

Islamist ideologist Sayyid Qutb writes, 'humanity today is living in a large brothel' with a 'mad lust for naked flesh', together with a 'system of usury which fuels man's voracity for money and engenders vile methods for its accumulation and investment'.[8] As in the German case, as von Treitschke describes it, pride in one's own character in reaction to the contempt of others is tied to contempt for them, which is what makes this sort of identity so dangerous when continuing clashes of culture foster this linkage.

What sort of political aspirations attend the identity of standing? The kind of separation that is demanded will vary from case to case, depending upon the situation of the identity's bearers. Mixed in among others they may, as many Muslims do, simply seek to be regulated according to their own norms – in the Muslim case through the Sharia. For to be regulated in accordance with someone else's threatens the expression and ultimately the existence of the identity. But where the bearers are largely separate territorially the aspirations will most likely be national ones, in the sense of seeking a separate state. Many Islamic fundamentalists aim at the restoration of the Caliphate through which the world-wide community of Muslims – the Umma – are governed together and separately from others. The reason this is not usually thought of as nationalism is that it is contrasted with the nationalisms of the separate states into which Muslims are divided, or with Arab nationalism based on a shared language. But this is really a conflict of nationalisms rather than a conflict between nationalism and religion, so that it is right to say that in the Islamic conception 'there can be no such thing as an individual and sovereign Islamic nation set apart from the rest of Islam: all Islam is a single nation.'[9]

Many authors seem to have linked *all* cases of cultural identity to what I call the identity of standing. Charles Taylor, for example, derives from Herder the idea that 'a *Volk* should be true to itself, that is its own culture. Germans shouldn't try to be second rate Frenchmen'; and he goes on to compare 'this new ideal of authenticity' with 'the idea of dignity' which he sees as related to 'the decline of hierarchical society', in which the notion of honour was 'intrinsically linked to inequalities'.[10] The demand for recognition by cultural groups that the ideal of authenticity inspires is, in my terms, a demand that their standing be acknowledged and respected. But Taylor is wrong, in my view, to presume that *all* cultural identities are of this character and, consequently, that their demands must have this sort of motivation. He is misled, I suggest, by choosing examples where this is so. But, I have argued, this is a feature of the circumstances in which those groups formed themselves – circumstances in which the ideal of authenticity was attractive precisely because it allowed a group to be first-rate at their own thing, rather than just second-rate or worse at somebody else's, as they had been contemptuously taken to be.

There is a prevalent confusion at work here which leads to the assumption that all demands for political recognition of whatever sort by groups betray that at least one aspect of their identity is identity as standing. It is a confusion between recognition and respect. But while identity as standing is a reaction to presumed lack of respect and may lead to demands for respect it need not do so, since those from whom recognition is demanded may themselves not be respected, so that their respect is scorned. Conversely, while recognition of some sort may be accorded to an identity group so that its political demands are met, respect may be withheld. It is, in fact self-respect that identity as standing seeks to secure, not necessarily the respect of others. There is, of course, a sense of recognition as the acknowledgement of merit which brings it close enough to respect for a thesaurus to group the words together as synonymous. But this is not the sense in which political recognition is claimed.

Again, there is a further confusion which perhaps strengthens the assumption that all identity groups incorporate identity as standing in view of their demands for political recognition, though it sometimes rests upon the assimilation of recognition claimed by a pre-existent group and the recognition required to bring the group into existence. Many authors, including Charles Taylor, believe that a given identity depends not just on its self-ascription but on acknowledgement by others.[11] Some, like Axel Honneth,[12] also think that, beyond acknowledgement, respect is required for this identity to be ascribed to oneself, since a sense of identity depends on its being a source of self-esteem. So an identity group would only exist on these views if the required recognition were forthcoming. Yet this confuses two groups from whom recognition may be sought. On the one hand there is the mutual recognition by members of the identity group of each others' shared identity. On the other hand there is the recognition claimed by such a group from members of other groups. But while the former is arguably required to constitute the group, it is the latter that is involved in claims to political recognition.

Identity as Centre

Identity as standing is, I want to say, different from another type of cultural identity, also sometimes characterised in terms of national character, namely, what I shall call identity as *centre*. Identity as centre, as I shall understand it, is a reaction to the threat of hollowness, of anomie, of the lack of principles in accordance with which one can guide one's life. Asserting such an identity is precisely finding guiding principles with which one can identify, so that one conceives one's behaviour in accordance with them as purposeful and autonomous rather than haphazard or heteronomous. Character can obviously be thought of as the possession of such principles, and the development of national character is the production of common principles among a group, whose members might, antecedently, have thought of themselves as in this respect different, regionally, religiously, by class or whatever. Notice, then, that identity as centre is putatively a collective form of what is often called 'practical identity' – 'that is, those features of a person that ground at least some of their reasons to act'.[13] And cultural identity is often conceived as always a form of this, always identity as centre.

Again I want to question this generalisation and insist that identity as centre is a specific response to particular circumstances. Examples of these include the position of indigenous peoples within a colonial state and thereby exposed to its quite different mores. Here individuals may, notoriously, become anomic, and one way out of this situation is to find a system of values which is given authority by its being shared with other members of the indigenous group, thus creating an identity as centre. Another quite different example, as I hinted a moment ago, is the incorporation of people into a national state. Here the hollowness to be filled may be that regarding their role as citizens of this state, so that they have a reason to discharge obligations to those with whom they might otherwise have felt no affinity. The values appealed to will, in this kind of case, be public values, whether of deference to leaders, of love of liberty, or whatever else might be taken to mark their national character.

The case for some form of political separation arising from the assertion of identity as centre is superficially similar to that from the assertion of identity as standing, namely to be regulated in accordance with one's own values. But underneath this similarity is a crucial difference, namely that, while, with an identity as standing, the point is that these values are one's *own* and not someone else's, in the case of identity as centre it is that they provide a clear action-guiding framework that needs protecting from disturbance. In the standing case a contrast with the values of others is essential, in the centre case it is not. For the insecurities that the different types of identity address are also different: the insecurity of having unrespected values, in the standing case, as against the insecurity of having no adequate norms at all, in the centre one. The two can be conflated quite easily if practical identity is thought of as a conception 'under which you value yourself . . . under which you find your life to be worth living and your actions worth undertaking'.[14] But the two aspects of valuing oneself and finding reasons for one's actions need disentangling. A member of a group constituted by identity as standing can value himself as such whether or not he really instantiates its distinguishing traits: his congratulatory self-conception can be delusory. Conversely his taking up the norms of his identity as centre may lead to no such glow if they are particularly demanding.

Now none of this implies that these two types of cultural identity cannot be combined, and the fact that they sometimes are may be what misleads many theorists into assuming that they are analytically the same. But the combination is, I suggest, a purely contingent one, dependent, on our bent twig model, upon a combination of circumstances which do not uncommonly occur together. A minority might find itself *both* despised *and* unsettled in its traditional way of life by a dominant majority, so that the identity its members assert has elements both of standing and of normative centre. The position of immigrant as well as indigenous groups is often of this sort; and a good deal of contemporary theorising is directed towards such cases. Nor should it be assumed that this sort of combination is accomplished because both types of identity then have the same cultural content: what we can take pride in as distinctive and what guides our actions can, however, be different. If the Irish identity can be viewed as a combination of this sort and if de Valera's famous 'dream speech' captures it, then on the one hand he celebrates the frugality which the English despised as poverty and on the other endorses what were Catholic norms of 'right living' as what should form the centre of national identity.[15] Talk of values here obscures how various values are, not all of them being directly action-guiding.

A more important point to stress is that, even if the values involved in identity as standing and identity as centre are the same, the two types of identity do not somehow collapse into one another. We can imagine the one having been present without the other, if we imagine away the relevant circumstances. This is an instance of the thesis for which I am arguing, that it is not cultural content that determines identity but its character as a reaction to circumstances: we can imagine the same identity with different cultural content so long as this is sufficient to group together in the same way those exposed to these circumstances. In fact the content of a cultural identity can change. In the case of the Québecois, for instance, 'since the abrupt decline of Catholicism, language has become the key national marker'.[16] What we may suspect from this example, though, is that, whether or not Québecois identity was previously an identity of centre, it no longer is. For while Catholicism is apt to provide a normative centre, language, except where it is cherished as revealing values indiscernible outside of it, is not.

It needs to be added that a group's circumstances may well change. This may occasion a change of identity, as when a group previously content within a multicultural state finds itself exposed to pressures that lead it to seek separation, and come to assert an identity which supports this move. It may equally, and perhaps much more often, occasion a change in the type of identity the group has, even though it is the same identity that is asserted. Thus a national group that started life with an identity as standing in response to humiliation by neighbours may grow in confidence and in international esteem. In these circumstances, I believe, identity may actually be quite fragile, which is why governments then often bring downward pressure on their people to build an identity as centre. The state's international policies or its domestic welfare programmes may require considerable loyalty or fraternity which only giving its members the reasons that spring from a shared normative centre can supposedly supply. But many other changes in circumstances can also lead to modification in the type of cultural identity that group members possess.

Identity as Face and as Affiliation

One difference that I noted between identity as standing and identity as centre is that the former essentially involves dissociation from other groups, in the form of a deliberate contrast with their identities, which the latter does not. Now it is a point often made against the culturalist conception of identity, which sees cultural content as what marks out identity groups, that in fact cultural content is selected simply to differentiate groups. In the words of Fredrick Barth, 'the critical focus from this point of view becomes the ethnic boundary that defines the group, not the cultural stuff that it encloses'.[17] This, I believe, is an oversimplification since not all identity formation has this differentiating function, though much does. I turn then to another type of cultural identity which does fall into this category, which I shall call identity as *face*. It is the identity someone has in virtue of adopting a particular persona, whose root meaning is the facial mask worn by actors in Greek and Roman drama to indicate which character they were playing. Identity as face, therefore, picks out who the bearer is to the world, how he is to be identified; and that self-evidently requires, whatever its motive, differentiation from others, and conspicuous differentiation at that.

The sort of insecurity against which identity as face contends is, then, the fear of facelessness, as we say, of becoming a faceless individual, anonymous, without distinguishing marks. The classic scenario for this is assimilation, whether of an immigrant minority, of a national group like the Québecois, or of independent nations confronted with, say, the pan-European project. What it is about threatened assimilation that evokes this reaction, rather than accommodation to it, will vary. It may be the difficulty of adaptation, loss of power or lack of it within a new dispensation, the unattractiveness, for a variety of reasons, of the assimilating culture, or whatever. What we should resist assuming is that the cause of the negative reaction is always the existence of a prior identity which would be lost. This may characterise some situations, but in others a clear-cut distinct identity will only emerge as part of the reaction, even though its alleged prior existence will usually be invoked. The type of identity to emerge from the situation, however, will, in my bent twig theory, be identity as face, for the bearers of identity will wish to emphasise, or to invent, clearly discernible points of difference.

The cultural content of identity as face will concern the way people look, their behavioural styles, their customs and, very commonly, their language. What is important here, of course, is not only differentiation from others but relative uniformity within the differentiated group. For just as members must, to acquire distinctiveness, be recognisable to others as different, so they must be recognisably the same in the sight of other members of the group. As an example of this twin phenomenon we see the way in which Muslim minorities in European countries – and especially their women – have both dressed distinctively and often played down regional differences in order to emphasise that it is indeed in virtue of being Muslims – whose women veil themselves and so on – that they are to be recognised as different by infidels and as the same by fellow believers. Here shared language is not an available marker, as it is for many indigenous minorities under assimilative pressures. But it is, I want to say, these external markers that are far more important in the scenario I am envisaging than any supposedly 'inner' features such as those that identity as centre draws upon. And the reason for this is that it is not necessarily a loss of belief, say, that is feared, but a loss of identity qua distinctiveness. The European offer of private belief and public assimilation does not address this worry.

Political demands supported by identity as face centre upon the preservation of the relevant markers of difference. Muslim insistence on wearing the headscarf in France, and emotional claims to retain the pound and imperial measures in Britain, are of a piece. The history, values or whatever that are appealed to in such cases should not lead us to mistake the identity as face involved as of a different type. It may, though, as I have indicated, be combined with another. Immigrant groups, for example, may be exposed to the risk of anomie as well as assimilation, and find a face which is a coherent expression of their centre. However, the crucial elements of culture to be protected in campaigns motivated by identity as face are its conspicuous differences, the possession of which allows members to think of themselves as distinctive and to treat others, in a not necessarily unfriendly way, as alien. The shallowness, as it were, of many of these markers may seem to stand in the way of a robust and reassured defence of them; and this, together with the Herderian ideology of a unitary system of deep cultural differences, leads to apparently more significant, if less conspicuous, differences being linked to them. This, I am arguing, is, in the simple case, deceptive, as can be seen from the persistence of difference even when what supposedly supports it, like religion, falls away.

We earlier noted a number of confusions surrounding the fact that the politics of identity involves claims for recognition. There are yet others arising from the assimilation of all identities to identity as face; or, to put it another way, to collapse all identity politics into the politics of difference, if this is understood as a politics essentially involving the affirmation of difference. But this is wrongly to regard all claims to recognition as what Charles Tilly calls 'existence claims',[18] namely as claims to be recognised as existing as a distinct group. Clearly this is part of what a group threatened with assimilation may wish to claim, but there is no reason to think it is part of what other groups want. Sometimes this is because they are already recognised as existing, but are, for example, treated with disdain in the way that may give rise to identity as standing. But even when this recognition is not forthcoming it need not be existence as a separate identity group for which recognition is claimed, but, for instance, recognition as having a particular political status – as a separate political entity, say, in the case of secessionist demands. For it may be that the criterion of distinct existence used by those from whom secession is sought would never allow them to concede it, even when political separation could, for other reasons, be granted. Thus political separation from the rest of Ireland was demanded by the Protestant majority in the Six Counties, when recognition as a distinct cultural group from other Irish people was not; and, indeed, could not have been without compromising its territorial claim over an area with a substantial Catholic minority.

There is, as I said, a widespread belief that *all* cultural identities are, like identity as face, of a differentiating kind. But, just as identity as standing contrasts with identity as centre in expressly marking some contrast, as the other does not, so identity as face similarly contrasts with what I call identity as *affiliation*. The insecurity to which this type of identity is a response is that of lacking a relevant relationship with other people, and what supplies that lack is supposedly some set of shared characteristics in virtue of which there can be such a relationship. It is a relationship in which I can feel at ease with others in it because they are, it seems, like me. It is a threatened absence of *sameness* that is involved, not of difference, and so there is no express differentiation sought, although, of course, such a differentiation will be achieved. The paradigm case in which this kind of insecurity is experienced is that of a diaspora people, whose accustomed relationships are imperilled by their circumstances, so that its members fear they will have no familiar association to which to belong. But other cases include rapid social change in which old allegiances dissolve and new ones are sought. Indeed this is taken by some theorists like Ernest Gellner[19] to be the situation in which modern nations developed to provide such foci of affiliation, and with them shared cultures to unite their members – though again one might expect this to be an overgeneralisation.

The demands of groups characterised by identity as affiliation will be the creation or preservation of social or political spaces within which they themselves, their relationships and the cultures that mediate them can flourish. These can stretch from claims for government assistance, special schools and so on, through to national independence. Cultural content is that which is taken to foster what is thought of as community. But language, as an example of this, plays a quite different role here than in the case of identity as face, even if in a given group the two types of identity are, owing to a combination of circumstances, amalgamated. For when a language serves identity as affiliation it does so just because it acts as a medium of relationships. It can act as such in the private sphere of these relationships without being used publicly, since this application, crucial with identity as face, is irrelevant here. It is differences of this kind between demands that often enable us to discern of what type a given cultural identity is, or, more likely, which type is predominant in a complex identity.

Not that it is always easy, I concede, to know quite how to locate identities. The key, I am suggesting, is to discover how people think of themselves as a group in response to the circumstances they are or have been in, as they perceive them to be. So another case of identity as affiliation may well be when people are thrown together in response to persecution, discrimination or shared disadvantage. The lines along which they group together are those along which they are victimised; and, if it is cultural identity, rather than class or racial identity, that is involved, then it will have been, in some sense, in virtue of cultural markers that they were picked on or neglected. Their need to assert a shared identity here has, as it were, an ulterior motive, which will be expressed in specific political claims to counter their injustices. But its character qua identity as affiliation will be reflected in those claims that seek to preserve relationships across the group. These are exemplified by Roma demands for shared sites, rather than dispersion among others in social housing, because individual defence depends upon community.

Identity as Home

Closely related to identity as affiliation is what I call identity as *home*, where one's home gives one's identity in the sense of where one is from, either literally or metaphorically. So the insecurity that gives rise to this identity is the threat of, in some sense, homelessness, either of lacking or losing a home, or of being unable to locate it. There are, I want to say, numerous cases of this – some so different that different types of identity might perhaps be postulated for them. But the typology I am constructing is, anyway, only a matter of convenience, revealing no hard and fast ontological categories, because the circumstances which give rise to the types of identity themselves are contingent and particular. To construct an ideal type here, then, is to find something common in the sort of reaction people have to a variety of situations – a way in which what seems menacing about each is to some extent the same. So we have to prescind from the fact that an actual home serve people's interests in shelter and succour to ask what is it about who I am that homelessness, in some sense, threatens.

What is involved is, I suggest, a sense that one lacks a

place in the world, and that can be supplied by an imagined place as much as by a real one, and a real one provides that place only as it is imagined. It is, then, a place where one belongs whose absence is feared, and what constitutes one's 'place' depends on how one imagines the world and one's relation to it. So an itinerant people will not typically think of a spatial location as providing it, rather than a place in a lineage or clan; while a sedentary group or one held together by folk memories of a sedentary past will focus on just that. But this last kind of group is precisely one of those that have collectively experienced dispossession or deracination, and these are among the circumstances to which this type of identity is a response. The severing of links with their past among people uprooted and forced by economic or political circumstances to move around within what we think of as the same territory can have a similar effect. Then for them to feel the need for a place in some common history is again a way of seeking a home. For an actual location can be regarded as a scene in a narrative, and whether this scene is important, or the continuity of the narrative is established otherwise through its key settings, will reflect how this type of identity as home can be constructed with different cultural materials.

A variety of circumstances and experiences, then, can lead to the fear of homelessness, as I understand it, and a range of cultural materials can be drawn upon to flesh out the type of identity that is a response. The political claims that identity as home supports will again vary depending upon the situation in which the identity group finds itself. If, like many indigenous peoples, they are threatened with loss of their land, or of sole occupancy of it, then a sense of their relation to it as constituting who they are is likely to develop and to lead to corresponding political claims for unrestricted possession. If, by contrast, they are a dispersed people, then their sense of a common identity may spring precisely from their belief in a common ancestral homeland, which may, as with Zionists, lead to political claims for its restoration, or, as with Rastafarians, remain a largely sentimental attachment that nonetheless generates claims to recognition as a distinct ethnic group. Or again, if it is internal mobility that gives rise to insecurity about people's place in their world then this may lead to demands either that others, such as immigrants, be excluded from the homeland that supplies that place, or that they make the people's history which provides it their own. And these examples could be multiplied.

Identity as home differs from identity as affiliation in being indirectly relational, in the sense that, unlike the latter, what collects the identity group together is their relation to a home in some sense of the notion, rather than their relation to the other members. Both types of identity can generate the feelings of being at home, either with one's fellows or in one's own place. In this respect they are related because being estranged and being unsettled are similar affective states. But they address, I suggest, different anxieties, even if these anxieties often occur together. Two other possible assimilations should also be resisted. One is to suppose that any identity whose content involves images of home is thereby of the type: identity as home. For pride in one's homeland as what has made one what one is, or as what one has made because of what one is, could be aspects of identity as standing, to give but one example. Conversely, if a people's identity depends heavily upon cultural content that involves their distinctive language or music, say, we should not automatically assume that it is identity as face that it articulates. For one way in which its members can create a home for themselves is to find it in their literature, or other art forms, through which their relation to the world can be imaginatively mediated. A home, as I hinted earlier, need be no real place or past, and even when it is, to be a home it must have the kind of imaginative appeal that makes one feel at home in it, rather than alienated from it or indifferent to it. Cultural content, as I have been maintaining, is not the key to what type of cultural identity a people possesses.

Having said that, though, we should expect identity as home to involve a place in some history. For what is sought is a settled place not just in the here and now, but in the unfolding of things, so that one can connect where one is, in common with others, to the place or places where one's predecessors as members of the group have been. A historical homeland is, in this sense, a more secure place than some accidental contemporary one – Israel, for the Jews, is more secure than the homeland in Uganda once mooted for them. And without an actual place, as I indicated earlier, a place in history whether by genealogy or some other narrative of continuity can fulfil a similar role; or, with one, reinforce it. Not, again, that history always performs this function. It may as easily provide cultural content for identity as standing, for example, by supplying praiseworthy models of national character.

Identity as Mission and as Mere Label

Identity as home is an answer to the question with which circumstances may confront people, 'where are you from?' But situations may also give to the question who someone is the force of 'what are you here to do?' as when he identifies himself at the door as the man who has come to mend the roof. So too a group may find itself having to ask itself what it is doing and find its shared identity in specifying a common purpose. This is what I shall call identity as *mission*. The classic example of such an identity would be a group of settlers, possibly of mixed origins, finding themselves in a land whose indigenous inhabitants do things differently from them and in ways to which they are unable or unwilling to assimilate. It is not just that the settlers have a common interest in solidarity with each other, though typically they do. It is that they see what is common to them in evaluative terms as bringing improvement to where they are, and it is the sharing of this project that leads them to think of themselves as having the same identity.

On the face of it this may seem a sub-case of identity as centre since some common action-guiding values are involved. But it is, I suggest, a distinct type of identity because it confronts a different challenge. This is not the problem of anomie, of a lack of guiding principles for individual members. It is, rather, a problem of specifying a common purpose, which is consistent with considerable variation in individual norms. What the purpose is intended to foster, then, is a certain sort of relationship with fellow members, namely of co-operation with them in the common project. Identity as centre, by contrast, does not have to do with such an intended communal relationship, but only with individual characteristics. Nor should that incline one to think that identity as mission is, instead, a sub-case of identity as affiliation. For it is not, as in that case, loneliness that threatens, but the absence of a certain sort of solidarity. Though in both cases, of course, the intended relationship may not materialise: the cultural identity may not produce a real community.

Settler groups are not the only kind to be bound together by identity as mission. What are thought of as national groups often have this type of identity as at least an important constituent of what their members think of as holding them together. Thus Mazzini maintained that, of the different nations, 'each has a post entrusted to it; each a special operation to perform; and the common victory [of humanity] depends on the exactness with which the different operations are carried out'.[20]

Similarly, certain sorts of religion can, as the word 'mission' suggests, lead their members to think of themselves as having a common identity, rather than simply sharing certain beliefs and practices, precisely because they have a common purpose to fulfil together. This may be an evangelising one, adding new members to the group by conversion, or it may be simply carrying out God's purposes in an environment of hostile unbelief. The former, in a secularised version, is what constitutes the mission of the cosmopolitan identities of groups promulgating liberal democracy, socialism or whatever. Again the scenario is of people brought together by the need to define themselves in terms of a common project against a background of others who are antagonistic or just set in their own ways.

The cultural content of identity as mission can, then, as this sketch suggests, be very various. It often involves histories from which future destinies can be projected; though here history is playing a different role than in identity as home, easily combinable with this type of identity as identity as mission is in appropriately complex circumstances. Broader world views, as in many religious and secular examples, can also play a part, and these may be expressed in literature, sacred or profane, philosophical and legal tracts, inspirational music and art, and so on. It is, to labour the point, the use to which such cultural materials are put that establishes the type of identity they serve, if any, not their specific content. And it is important here to distinguish their use simply to express individual beliefs and aspirations from their use to constitute a type of identity. For, I am maintaining, it is only in particular sorts of circumstance that people who share beliefs will think of themselves as sharing an identity in virtue of this. Identity as mission is a type of identity that sometimes illustrates this kind of progression.

The political aims of groups defined in terms of identity as mission are similarly various. In the national case the claim to separate statehood is justified as what is needed to fulfil the national mission. What I called settler groups are often a subclass of this case, claiming political control of a territory to effect improvement, despite its prior occupation by others. Religious groups may seek only the freedom to pursue their mission, since without it not only their mission but their existence as a group with this type of identity is threatened. Secular evangelisers may have analogous or more ambitious goals, of which the attempt to influence the constitutions of states whose members may not already profess the preferred identity is an obvious example. The justification is that without such constitutions the inhabitants of these states will be unable to achieve the designated identity as mission. But this overlooks, of course, the fact that with such constitutions in place other kinds of identity – a Muslim identity as affiliation, for example – may become more difficult or impossible.

Identity as mission, it may be felt, is not so clearly a response to a specific sort of insecurity as the other types of identity I have mapped out, and this can to some extent be conceded. Without such an identity, I have suggested, a group of people may experience a lack of a common purpose, a reason to act together. In certain hostile situations this is to feel a kind of isolation – not the isolation of loneliness, but rather the isolation of a lack of solidarity. Again, the situation of isolated settlers may be imagined to dramatise the sort of insecurity involved, and then the way in which identifying with others in the same situation can allay it may be understood. This is, I suggest, a model of the way groups defined by an identity as mission think of their position, even when it is difficult to discover the kinds of real danger that settlers often face. The Western as a parable for the civilising mission of America illustrates the point.

There is, however, a general moral to be drawn from this sort of case. When actual insecurities are allayed, at least in part by the adoption of the relevant type of identity, then that identity, as a response to such insecurities, is itself in danger. It may, as I hinted earlier, become quite fragile and require buttressing by fables of threat, as for example by the supposed threat to liberal democracy of Islamic extremism, or need replacing with another type of identity with a similar extension but more appropriate to changed circumstances. There is, though, a degenerate type of identity encountered in such situations which I shall call identity as *label*. Here people resort to identifying themselves as they do simply to have some answer to the question who they are. And this, I suggest, is what many of the types of identity I have mentioned turn into when the circumstances that create them pass. Conversely mere labels, I am claiming, should be investigated for their origins in such initiating circumstances. Only then, according to the bent twig theory, will the extent and shape of the identity become apparent.

However, nothing I have said should be taken to imply that all those who think of themselves in terms of the nondegenerate types of identity I have itemised must feel the reactive emotions that give rise to them. That they do not does not turn their identities into mere labels. For that to happen, I want to say, the discourse that originally sustained their identity must have lost its power much more widely. It is no doubt true that identities are initially shaped by a vanguard group and are then found compelling as self descriptions by the broader constituency to whom they are ascribed. Nor should it be thought that the reactive emotions of such a constituency would have been available without the discourses that this vanguard composed. Indeterminate dissatisfaction with the circumstances that a number of people face is given shape as a specific reactive emotion by these discourses and they are thereby formed into a group with a particular type of identity. Even if the circumstances do not touch them personally, they are still able to experience the feeling imaginatively and make the corresponding identification. The identity becomes a mere label only when this experience ceases to be accessible.

The sort of investigation I have been conducting should not be taken to provide a systematic typology of cultural or, more narrowly, national identity. But enough has perhaps been done to cast doubt on the common assumption that cultural identity is, as national character was thought to be, a unitary phenomenon. Furthermore, the fact that the features of the different types embody responses to different circumstances and give rise to varying political demands should lead us to be suspicious of those metaphysical accounts of identity that try to relate them logically, rather than contingently and mutably. Cultural identity, and with it national identity, are essentially political concepts deployed to support political claims – in the national case of a right to political autonomy. The idea that there is a pervasive system of deep going cultural differences, such as Herder held, is a convenient and rhetorically persuasive one in this regard, as was the theory of national character. It would take more argument to show that it is no more than that. All I have tried to do here is to show that the bent twig approach to classifying distinct types of cultural identity offers a plausibly sceptical alternative.

Scepticism, of course, usually seems wildly counter intuitive. But in this case that is, I want to say, because the Herderian picture of different sorts of people has acquired such a hold over us that, with the passing of naturalistic explanations of difference, culturalist ones were grasped at to fill the gap. Then individual identity seemed to have an ontological character of which culture is an aspect. But in fact we should not really expect identity to be a single thing anyway or, consequently, for 'cultural identity' to have a single denotation. For when we ask someone's identity we do so in different contexts in which different sorts of answer are in order, giving one's official, professional, familial, communal identity, or whatever, depending upon the purpose for which the question is asked and the knowledge one's interlocutor possesses. And the same holds when one asks the question of oneself. I may be concerned about what distinguishes me from others or what relates me to them, with what gives me some status or with what my wellspring of action is. And these, I have suggested, parallel some of the kinds of question that collections of people are forced to answer in the circumstances they are placed in. But there is no reason to think that some overarching answer is available to them, derived from the existence of some item with a complex ontological character.

This is, indeed, where even the bent twig model finally fails, for bent twigs are all different shaped twigs, and twigs do have some ontological character. But different types of cultural identity, as I have termed them, are only all cultural identities in a nominal sense. In all seeming to answer the same question, 'who are you?', by alluding to cultural characteristics they acquire a spurious unity which disappears when we realise that the question 'who?' can be intended in many different ways. The bent twig is, then, a useful metaphor, not to be pressed too far. The danger of the bent twig springing back and inflicting injury is, however, one aspect of the metaphor worth exploring, but that is a matter for a later chapter.

Notes

1. David Miller, 'Crooked timber or bent twig? Berlin's nationalism', in G. Crowder and H. Hardy (eds), *The One and the Many: Reading Isaiah Berlin* (New York, NY: Prometheus Books, 2007).
2. Quoted in ibid. p. 182, n. 3.
3. Isaiah Berlin, *Against the Current: Essays in the History of Ideas* (London: Hogarth Press, 1979), p. 12.
4. Isaiah Berlin, *The Roots of Romanticism* (Princeton, NJ: Princeton University Press, 2001), p. 131.
5. Due to Theodor Schieder. See Ulf Hedetoft, 'National rituals of belonging', in G. H. Herb and D. H. Kaplan (eds), *Nations and Nationalism: a Global Historical Overview* (Santa Barbara, CA: ABC-CLIO, 2008), pp. 501–3.
6. Paul Robinson, *Military Honour and the Conduct of War* (New York, NY: Routledge, 2006), p. 3.
7. Heinrich von Treitschke, quoted in Liah Greenfeld, *Nationalism* (Cambridge, MA: Harvard University Press, 1992), pp. 377–8.

8. Sayyid Qutb, quoted in Malise Ruthven, *Fundamentalism* (Oxford: Oxford University Press, 2004), p. 37.
9. Thomas Kiernan, *The Arabs* (London: Sphere, 1975), p. 200.
10. Charles Taylor, *Multiculturalism* (Princeton, NJ: Princeton University Press, 1994), pp. 31, 27.
11. 'Our identity is partly shaped by recognition or its absence, often by the *mis*recognition of others', ibid. p. 25. Here the absence of recognition seems to mean some form of disrespect, as the coinage 'misrecognition' suggests. While this could be taken to imply that disrespect triggers identity as standing, it also apparently indicates that *some* form of recognition, even misrecognition, is required for identity.
12. See Axel Honneth, *The Struggle for Recognition* (Cambridge: Polity, 1995).
13. Matthew Festenstein, *Negotiating Diversity* (Cambridge: Polity, 2005), p. 10.
14. Christine M. Korsgaard, *The Sources of Normativity* (Cambridge: Cambridge University Press, 1996), p. 101.
15. See P. Craig (ed.), *The Oxford Book of Ireland* (Oxford: Oxford University Press, 1998), p. 13.
16. James Kennedy, 'Québec', in Herb and Kaplan, *Nations and Nationalism*, p. 1296.
17. Fredrick Barth, 'Ethnic groups and borders', in J. Hutchinson and A. D. Smith (eds), *Ethnicity* (Oxford: Oxford University Press, 1996), p. 79.
18. Charles Tilly, *The Politics of Collective Violence* (Cambridge: Cambridge University Press, 2003), p. 201.
19. See Ernest Gellner, *Thought and Change* (London: Weidenfeld and Nicolson, 1964), ch. 7.
20. Joseph Mazzini, *The Duties of Man* (London: Dent, 1907), p. 55.

5

The Embodiment of Cultural Identity

The Case of Madame Silmi

Faiza Silmi is a Moroccan woman, married to a French citizen, who has lived in France since 2000 and has four children who are French citizens by birth.[1] She applied for French citizenship herself but her application was refused by the Conseil d'État on the grounds that although she

> possesses a good command of the French language, she has nonetheless adopted a radical practice of her religion incompatible with the essential values of the French community and notably with the principle of equality between the sexes.[2]

The practice in question is the wearing of a *burqa* that reveals only the eyes, which, Mme Silmi contends, is her own choice. The reason for the denial of citizenship, then, is that she has assimilated insufficiently into French culture. The precise character of her Muslim identity is, it is supposed, incompatible with the kind of cultural identity required for French citizenship.

One of the interesting aspects of this case is first of all that it is a marker of bodily difference, an item of clothing, that disqualifies Mme Silmi as culturally too discrepant. But, secondly, as if this were not by itself enough to mark a significant difference, the item of clothing is taken to express deep-going features of identity: no less, in fact, than the bearer's values. It is not, I think, as some observers have supposed, the suspicion that Mme Silmi's husband, himself of Moroccan descent, imposed the *burqa* on her that is the relevant factor here. Indeed the fact that she herself chose to wear it is essential to the Conseil d'État's argument, for only then would it be expressive of her supposedly divergent values. These values are taken to be those that stem from a particular reading of the Quran that stresses such verses as:

> Men are the managers of the affairs of women . . . Righteous women are therefore obedient . . . And those you fear may be rebellious admonish; banish them to their couches, and beat them.[3]

These values would indeed be incompatible with at least the publicly proclaimed values of French society. But it should go without saying that any inference to them from the wearing of the *burqa* is very questionable. For such modes of dress might just as easily signal a rejection of Western attitudes to women as publicly exposed sex objects. This cultural incompatibility, however, would presumably not be disqualificatory.

What is actually involved here is not my present concern. Rather I am interested in the picture of the relation between the body and cultural identity that it encapsulates. It is a picture by no means confined to the French, though its Cartesian character makes its French exemplification particularly apt. For the picture is of a person's identity being constituted by her beliefs – in this case her ethical ones. Her body, by contrast, is simply an object like any other in the world, but one from whose behaviour, and the appearance she has given it, her beliefs can be inferred, because its behaviour and acquired appearance are a consequence of her will. This Cartesian dichotomy in which each person is essentially *res cogitans* – a thinking thing – whose beliefs make her who she is, on the one hand, with, on the other hand, a body that indicates her identity, it is this that infects, I suggest, all accounts of cultural identity that construe it in terms of *psychological* differences between people. In particular it lurks beneath those accounts that see cultural identity as a species of practical identity, classifying people by the different beliefs that ground their actions.[4]

Like all Cartesian theories, this picture is attractive partly because it sees a person's identity as in principle accessible to her. She has but to reflect upon her beliefs to find out who she is, and, as far as her cultural identity is concerned, to see with what group of people's beliefs the relevant ones coincide. There may be an element of choice here, of course, but then judgement is under the control of the will in the Cartesian picture. The important point is that on the kind of account of cultural identity we are discussing, while I may go wrong in my classification of my identity because I can go wrong about other people's, I have the materials for being right about my own in the shape of my relevant beliefs. That is why on this kind of account identity and its self-ascription are generally taken to coincide. The fact that I have a certain identity and that I think of myself as having this identity are taken to coincide because I supposedly have a privileged access to those wellsprings of action, those psychological features of myself, in which my identity consists. If I am not as fully cognisant of my cultural identity as leaders of the cultural group would wish then, on this commonplace picture, they have only to adjure me to reflect upon these features to get me to acknowledge it, or, if I am so minded, to reject it by a determination of the will.

Now there is no denying that in some situations the facts of the case seem to support the application of this picture, and Mme Silmi's may well be an example. For she seems to have reflected upon her beliefs, made her choice among the options open to her, and then adapted her behaviour and appearance specifically to express the identity she took herself to have as a consequence of this. She no doubt also intended that others would read off from her wearing of the *burqa* a fundamentalist Muslim identity, though, as I have said, any inference to a rejection of sexual equality in some form is much more precarious. But this case is surely exceptional. For the most part people do not choose the type of clothing they wear; still less do they choose it with the intention of signalling some belief. I may choose to wear jeans rather than a pair of grey flannels, but nothing much about my deep-seated beliefs can be read from this, at most a preference for the casual and the demotic rather than the more formal and classy. I do not, however, choose to wear trousers rather than a dhoti or a sarong: it is just that I have been brought up in a country where trousers are worn rather than in rural India or Malaya. Something can be inferred about my culture, then, in a broad sense of the term; but my trousers say nothing about my identity, not because they express no belief, but because they have not been accorded the role of marking an identity.

This is not the place to expose the errors of the Cartesian account.[5] It is enough to assert that we are essentially embodied beings, so that insofar as we are shaped by our cultures it is in our bodies that we are affected, and not only indirectly so through the mediation of our minds. It is one thing, however, to make this very general claim about the way our bodies manifest culture, quite another, I believe, to view this as the manifestation of cultural *identity*. For talk of identity is a highly specific discourse in which the question addressed is who someone is. From their culture is extracted part of an answer to this question; it is not mentioned merely to explain certain facts about them, as his being Malay and thus participating in Malayan culture might explain his wearing a sarong. Rather he might be identified as a Malay in virtue of, among other things, his wearing a sarong. It is certain specific cultural features and not just any features of someone's culture that play this particular role. What we are interested in, then, is how some of these bodily features may do this, how, that is, the body can play the role of marking an identity.

The Body for Oneself and the Body for Others

As part of their critique of the Cartesian picture both Merleau-Ponty and Sartre introduce a valuable distinction between the body-for-oneself and the body-for-others. Sartre explains 'these two modes of being which we find for the body' as follows:

> Being-for-itself must be wholly body and it must be wholly consciousness; it can not be *united* with a body. Similarly being-for-others is wholly body; there are no 'psychic phenomena' there to be united with the body. There is nothing *behind* the body. But the body is wholly 'psychic'.[6]

To take the body-for-oneself first, Sartre's argument is that I do not of course experience my body, as Descartes' picture would have us believe, as an object like any other. In writing, for example, it is the pen I watch, 'but my hand has vanished'; 'the body is inapprehensible, it does not belong to the objects in the world'. My body, Sartre goes on, is 'the point of view on which there can not be a point of view' because it is 'a conscious structure of my consciousness' of the world. Insofar as I can be conscious of my body this is like being conscious of a sign when all that I attend to is the sign's meaning. Yet though in this situation consciousness of the body is, as Sartre puts it, retrospective, at others the body forces itself upon my attention. For example, 'at the very moment that I am reading *my eyes hurt'*. But here too Sartre stresses, pain is 'not referred back to a body-for-others. It is the eyes-as-pain';[7] that is to say, it is the eyes that are experienced as painful, rather than pain being experienced and then located in a part of the body as it is identified by others. My own relation to my body is quite different.

The body-for-me, however, is conditioned in the way in which I can be conscious of the world through it by contingent facts about my body. Unlike the Cartesian body which is a mere addition to the mind, how the world can appear to me is dependent on such facts, as Sartre interestingly observes, that I am 'French or German or English, etc., a proletarian or aristocrat, etc., weak and sickly or vigorous, irritable or of amiable disposition'. My race, class, nationality, disposition and so on are indicated as giving 'my point of view on the world by the world itself',[8] that is to say, by the way various avenues are open or closed to me, by the way others relate to me, by the way certain things and places engage my attention, and so on. This is not, of course, for Sartre a deterministic picture: there is always scope for choice. That choice operates within parameters set by the physical conditions of my bodily existence. But these conditions within which I operate, Sartre observes, are not known to me except by my taking another's standpoint upon myself. For example, 'character has a distinct existence only in the capacity of an object of knowledge for the Other. Consciousness does not know its own character.'[9] And this leads Sartre to deny that character can be distinguished from the body, as against its being some psychic entity.

We can now see, then, what Sartre understands as the body-for-others. It involves someone's body being viewed as an object, though this is not the primary way in which I encounter him, namely as one for whom it is I that am the object. But still I do not, as Sartre puts it, 'perceive the other's body as flesh',[10] for it is always replete with meaning in the sense of having that relation to things around it which bespeaks the other person's commerce with the world. When I am aware of myself as a body-for-others in the way someone looks at me I realise, Sartre says, that as an object I am 'an unknowable being', alienated from myself because I cannot control how I am seen. This experience is manifest in embarrassment, shyness and so forth. Yet this experience is troubling only because 'the body-for-the-Other *is* the body-for-us, but inapprehensible and alienated'.[11] To take up the other's point of view on oneself, however, does not resolve the problem, for there is still a gap between that and the way we experience the body-for-us.

While Merleau-Ponty's account of the distinction has many similarities to Sartre's it differs somewhat in relation to these last points. The situation in which I experience myself as an object under the gaze of another is, Merleau-Ponty insists, an exceptional case:

> In fact the other's gaze transforms me into an object, and mine him, only if both of us withdraw into the core of our thinking nature, if we both make ourselves into an inhuman gaze, if each of us feels his actions not taken up and understood, but observed as if they were an insect's. This is what happens, for instance, when I fall under the gaze of a stranger.[12]

For the most part, however, we 'find the communication between one consciousness and another in one and the same world'.[13] This Merleau-Ponty characterises as a cultural world in which the meanings of each other's actions are transparent to them so that they share a common ground on which to interact. Then 'the "for me" and the "for others" co-exist in one and the same world'.[14] Merleau-Ponty thinks of a recognition of the union of these within oneself, presumably a pre-reflective one manifest in unselfconscious action, as necessary for one to respond to other people's bodies as other than insect-like.

It would be wrong to overemphasise the contrast between Sartre and Merleau-Ponty here, for, as I indicated, Sartre too notes that I do not primarily perceive the other as an object. Nevertheless, we can draw on the contrast to make what I think is a useful distinction between two notions. First, there is what I shall term the obtrusive body-for-others, as someone else's body might appear to me as a stranger to his activity, or as I experience mine when I am embarrassed under the gaze of another. Second, there is the unobtrusive body-for-others, as when the body is not specifically focused on because it is the action that is the object of attention in the ordinary shared activities of life. This is, then, a specialised use of the term 'obtrusive', in which, for example, a bright yellow safety vest does not necessarily make its wearer in my sense an obtrusive body-for-others, since it may still be the way he signals me to stop or the like that I am led to concentrate upon. Rather, however muted its colour, the sarong that I wear to work one day will almost certainly make me an obtrusive body-for-others, for colleagues will be distracted from what I am doing by my unaccustomed bodily appearance and I am likely to feel ill at ease myself.

I shall use the resulting threefold distinction in conjunction with the idea of a cultural body, that is to say a body shaped in its appearance and styles of behaviour by broadly speaking cultural factors rather than biological ones. This contrast, however, is not clear cut, for biological features like skin or hair colour can have cultural meanings, so that their conspicuous display can be either cultivated or occluded by their bearers. In this case they can be regarded as cultural features too. We have already encountered the cultural body-for-ourselves in Sartre's remarks about the way in which what he terms 'nationality' conditions my body just as my physiology does, so that I experience my physical activity in the world in a particular way. Merleau-

Ponty, too, stresses that one's world is a cultural world and we can illustrate the distinction between the obtrusive and the unobtrusive body-for-others from one of his examples, doubtful though it is anthropologically. For, he maintains,

> the behaviour associated with anger or love is not the same in a Japanese and an Occidental. Or, to be more precise, the difference in behaviour corresponds to a difference in the emotions themselves . . . The angry Japanese smiles, the westerner goes red and stamps his foot or else goes pale and hisses his words.[15]

Now we can easily see in such cases how within one's own culture the expressive body remains unobtrusive, while when one confronts someone from another we encounter in him the obtrusive body-for-others.

The Formation of Identities

It may be thought that the foregoing trichotomy yields a fairly simple non-Cartesian view of cultural identity. Mme Silmi's problem, it might be thought, is that she cannot be part of 'the French community' because, shrouded in her *burqa*, her body-for-others remains irremediably obtrusive, however unobtrusive it would be in some Muslim societies. Her body-for-self similarly inhabits a different world, unable in public to respond to the facial expression of others reciprocally. She is thus doubly excluded, it might be said, from French communal interactions. But in both respects her exclusion is essentially due to embodied features of her cultural identity, not to any inferred psychological ones. If the Conseil d'État were both honest and uninfected by Cartesianism, it would give this as the reason for denying her French nationality. For, at least in a republic such as France is, it may be regarded as necessary to participate in the sort of communal interactions which the way she presents herself to others precludes. Then, if we are to criticise the decision, it may be thought that this requires a critique of French republicanism as unsuitable for a multi-cultural society. This is not the place to pursue this line, but the unexamined picture of cultural identity it involves does require further discussion.

First, it employs a view of objective cultural differences conferring distinct identities on people. But this is not what it is to have an identity, something which gives an answer to the question who one is. For an identity must be, to state it baldly, something with which I can identify myself, both in the sense of providing my answer to the question and in that of my accepting it as what I am. Though the Cartesian picture misconstrues the coincidence between one's iden-tity and its self-ascription it is right to see a connection here. While an individual may for a variety of reasons be ignorant of or misguided about her identity, that she has the identity depends upon her being able to ascribe it to herself in the way that very many of those with the same identity already do. It is clear that Mme Silmi fulfils this condition and also that, in describing her wearing of the *burqa* as part of a religious practice which she has 'adopted', the Conseil d'État rests its case upon her doing so. It rests its case upon her identifying herself in a way supposedly incompat-ible with a French identity. But this does not take us back to psychological features. Rather, one might suggest, her self-identification consists in her taking on the type of body-for-self that she does, including among other things the wearing of the *burqa*, rather than attempting to mould herself to another.

It is tempting here to say the Mme Silmi feels at home in this body, clad in its *burqa*. But, and this is my second point, that would be in danger of assimilating all cultural identities and their associated forms of embodiment to a single model. This, however, as I have argued earlier, over-looks the fact that it is only in particular social and political circumstances that people need to ascribe themselves an identity. When they do so they are addressing the question who they are in different senses depending upon those circumstances. Thus it is natural that a Muslim uprooted from her own community, with its particular mores shaped, partly, by religion, should feel out of place in a society like that of France. For her to ask the question 'Who am I? Who am I here?' is in these circumstances to invite an answer which supplies the place in the world she takes herself to have. One answer is, of course, to make oneself at home, as we say, in France, but this may be difficult or undesirable. Another will be an answer shared by many with the same reactions and it is likely to draw upon common cultural materials deriving from their original community. Among these will be bodily styles, of dress, demeanour and so forth in which one can feel at ease. And this will involve not feeling that one is an obtrusive body-for-others. One may be exactly that, but one will not have the sort of feelings of embarrassment, awkwardness and so forth that this can bring, because one is secure in the identity to which one's body-for-self conforms.

This case is, I want to say, only one possibility. That someone has what I call identity as home – identifying herself by her place in the world, given by a variety of cultural materials – is, to repeat, dependent upon her finding herself in the appropriate circumstances, or at least on her being a member of a group many of whose members find themselves in these circumstances and experience the feelings of homelessness to which this sort of identity is a response. It is, then, only if this is the type of identity that Mme Silmi ascribes to herself that we should expect her to feel at home in her body, for only then will the shape she gives it be a component of her identity as home. None of this implies that otherwise she does not feel at home in her body. It is just that, if she does, this need have nothing to do with her identity as expressed by her *burqa* and so on.

Indeed it is possible that she feels ill at ease in it, exposed to others as an obtrusive body-for-others. No doubt she would resent this, but carry on defiantly in her chosen demeanour. The situation would, of course, be different among members of her own group. But that, it seems to me, is as likely a scenario for her in the streets of France as the preceding one, so that she is, even under her protective garment, not at home there, and anxious to return to places and people where she does not experience this sensation, an unobtrusive body-for-others there.

Yet again she may not retreat. Her defiance, as I have termed it, may lead to a different reaction. She may actually wish to be an obtrusive body-for-others in French public places. Whether she feels at home or not in her body-for-self is then immaterial. This, I suggest, is the situation when the identity she ascribes to herself is what I call identity as face. It is, we may say, the identity that provides that answer to the question who one is which indicates how one is to be identified by others. The face in a passport photo does this job. Mme Silmi's face is, however, concealed by her *burqa*, so it is not as an individual that she is identifying herself but as a member of a group, as undeniably a practising Muslim woman. In this identity she marks out her difference from the other women about her in France, and for this it is crucial that she does appear as an obtrusive body-for-others. The circumstances which induce someone to ascribe this identity to themselves are those in which they, or other members of their group, fear 'facelessness' – fear, that is to say, assimilation in which they will no longer have a distinct collective identity. And they reject it by emphasising points of conspicuous difference, for which the body in its appearance and mode of interaction with other bodies provides an obvious site for cultural differentiation.

The obtrusiveness of the body-for-others in such a situation may have other effects. For its obtrusiveness may make it unreadable, in the way that the unobtrusive body-for-others is readable through expressing purposes, feelings, attitudes and so forth. A literal example of the body's unintelligibility is an unknown foreign tongue – sounds from the mouth which obtrude upon one as strange noise, without meaning. And that this is not how immigrants should appear publicly is the demand that they speak the natives' language – a demand, we noticed, with which Mme Silmi was able and willing to comply, since for her distinct identity as face is not constructed in terms of a different language, even though many such identities are. Islam, however, spans a variety of language groups, classical Arabic having special significance only as the language in which the Prophet dictated the Quran, not as a language of ordinary speech. Merleau-Ponty's example of the Japanese smiling when angry would be another example of unreadability. For his Occidental would not know what to make of it, assuming that they did not misread it as an expression of pleasure; they would scrutinise the face and see it only as part of an obtrusive body-for-others. But in ordinary circumstances this is no part of a Japanese identity, in the way in which a woman's wearing a kimono abroad might be. It is simply how the Japanese act, with no thought of others' reactions.

The Embodiment of Values

I have given here two types of identity, asserted, I want to say, in response to different sorts of circumstance, and I have given Mme Silmi's *burqa* as an example that could express either type. This is not to say that it may not express both. For she, like many other Muslim immigrants, may feel both the homelessness, as I termed it, that is felt in an unwelcoming society and the demand to assimilate that threatens facelessness, from which their current collective resemblance protects them. The circumstances conducive both to identity as home and to identity as face may each be present together and then the composite identity may be asserted too, so that the body plays both roles in expressing it. In other situations this will not be the case. Suppose, for example, an immigrant group's members are content to wear their traditional clothes and so on only in a private, domestic or religious setting rather than in public. This may be sufficient to satisfy the desire for an identity as home, leaving the streets a perhaps uneasy place for someone, not feeling at home in her body-for-self, dressed European style, but at least not presenting an obtrusive body-for-others. Yet this, of course, cannot satisfy a desire for identity as face, which requires conspicuous public difference – precisely what the French republican requirement for a public/private divide cannot permit. But if the circumstances for asserting an identity as face are absent, if, say assimilation is not pressed upon people so that they have no strong motive to differentiate themselves, then this public/private contrast in practice may be acceptable.

Conversely, the circumstances for asserting an identity as face may be present without those that seem to demand an identity as home. A people living in their own place but threatened by assimilation into some larger unit may experience this situation and respond to it by ritual appearances in national dress, folk dancing and so forth. The situation of the Baltic States within the Soviet Union exemplified this, with women wearing their characteristic coronas, gathered skirts and white stockings. Here the intention was to present obtrusive bodies-for-others – particularly for Russians – as bearers of a distinct identity, rather than simply to carry on old traditional customs which provided distinctive scope for the body-for-self. Here it is worth nothing that identity as face, in emphasising difference, deliberately presents a *mask*. The obtrusive body-for-others is, as I have noted, precisely an unexpressive body, in the way an unobtrusive body-for-others is not. Thus it is strangeness to others that needs to be utilised and that strangeness conceals, as the *burqa* literally conceals, what the strangely dressed or bizarrely behaving person is like. It was rash for the French Conseil d'État to read off from a body that its members did not understand anything about its bearer's attitudes that the Conseil terms her 'values'. They might, by contrast, have read off from the female French bodies acceptable and unobtrusive to them assertions of sexual equality or, perhaps, acceptance of inequality.

The point towards which I am moving is to insist that neither type of embodied identity I have sketched has anything to do with a person's values, and thus neither has anything to do with what is often called a person's 'practical identity'[16] – what it is about them in virtue of which they have the reasons for action that they do. Thus what the Conseil d'État alleged about Mme Silmi could be construed as a claim that her practical identity was incompatible with that required for full participation in French society. This type of identity in its collective cultural form is what I call identity as centre. For this type of identity, as I am understanding it, is a response to the fear of hollowness, of a lack of fixed principles of action. The circumstances that give rise to this kind of anxiety are multifarious, but one situation is indeed that of immigrants plunged into a society with mores very different from their original ones but to which they are expected to conform. Then how they are to act in any particular case and how the different norms are to be squared may indeed be problematic. One solution will be for them to adopt an identity in which what constitute the norms by which they should live, which constitute, as we say, their moral centre, are clear. So the question 'Who am I?' to which this identity supplies an answer is the inner directed one: 'Who am I to be?'

Thus the body-for-self is moulded to an identity as centre in more or less obvious ways. Wearing the *burqa*, for example, is an extreme symbol of the value set on women's modesty; for the Muslim woman is chaste, dignified, self-respecting and modest, while the woman who is ignorant of the divine guidance may be vain, showy, and anxious to display her attractions. Such display includes exposing the attractive parts of the body, walking and talking in a seductive manner, displaying her ornaments, wearing revealing and sexy clothes and the like,[17]

as one Muslim commentator, al-Qaradawi, puts it. On the face of it this seems to present us with the Cartesian picture of inner beliefs, stemming or not stemming from 'divine guidance', and a body fashioned to express them. And it is no doubt with some vague assumption of identity as centre being that which is expressed in Mme Silmi's appearance that the Conseil d'État made its inference to the unsuitability of her values for French citizenship. Indeed the adoption of a *burqa* in France can be construed on this model.

However, a closer scrutiny of al-Qaradawi's description of 'the Muslim woman' reveals a rather different picture. It is not conceivable that one would know how to comport oneself just on the basis of espousing values of chastity, dignity, self-respect and modesty. Al-Qaradawi provides an indication of how not to behave from his contrasting portrayal of the Western woman; but it is a body-for-others that is described, precisely because its features arise from her being 'showy, and anxious to display her attractions'. This is, in some respects, an obtrusive body-for-others, in particular for men. For the intention is that their responses to the ordinary expression of behaviour of the woman's body should be interrupted by views of it as an object, an object designed to have a particular effect on them. This is what the Muslim woman is to avoid. She is to avoid it by choosing as her body-for-self one that moves and presents itself in ways that are chaste, dignified and modest. But these are traits of bodily behaviour, not expressions of inner beliefs as the wearing of a *burqa* may be. As such they must be acquired quite differently, through bodily adjustments by means of which she becomes conscious of the world and others in it in a particular way. And this is a very different way from that in which al-Qaradawi's Western woman is conscious of them.

Bodily behaviour is, then, itself a mode of consciousness, not an effect of it. The way one moves, whether with eyes modestly downcast or boldly uplifted, and how one views the world coincide. But a belief in the value of modesty, say, is precisely a disposition to view the world in the former way. This sort of story is what leads Sartre to say that character exists only as an object of knowledge for the other, since it is the way I behave as an unobtrusively expressive body for others that determines what my character is, whether I am, for example, really modest or not. I aim to move in the right way – to have the appropriate body-for-self – to achieve this result. But my body is not an instrument (as the *burqa* is) with which I can do so, for I cannot witness my own body in this way. In fact, the way the body styles that determine character are acquired is usually by the imitation of models of the desired character, utilising the power of mimicry which we all possess and which, unreflectively, has led to our having our original bodies-for-self in the way Sartre spells out. For these are, in Sartrian terms, the result of pre-reflective choices in 'a world of already established corporal styles',[18] as Judith Butler puts it in discussing this point in respect to gender.

On the Sartrian picture even cultural identity as centre should not be conceived in the Cartesian way. The fear of anomie to which it is a response is principally an anxiety about how one's body-for-self should be directed. But that it is directed in a coherent way does not imply an inner director, just that one's body should be conformable to corporeal norms. It is only when these get codified, as in prescriptions for dress, that the inner/outer picture becomes appealing. But then it is clear that this is a secondary, derivative case, not the primary one. The codification of certain corporeal norms is a different matter from some being designated as markers of cultural identity. For most of the norms by which our bodies are regulated do not have this role; they merely reflect the way we are brought up to behave, and cultural stereotypes are ascribed partly on the basis of them; so that some groups are seen as dirty, noisy or whatever as a result of divergences from the observer's norms. Some corporeal norms, however, are picked out to embody those desirable character traits that constitute an identity as centre. The modest demeanour of Muslim women is, we have seen, one example. Another quite differently embodied modesty is that of the English gentleman, supposedly a model of national character, whose bearing deliberately contrasts with the braggadocio attributed to foreign nations. And many other body styles associated with other designated identity traits could be cited.

Parameters of Appearance

Mention of other-ascribed stereotypes as against self-ascribed moral traits brings us to a distinction we have utilised but not explicitly commented upon, namely that between the way the body appears to fellow members of an identity group and how it appears to non-members. The distinction is an important one for a number of reasons. The first is that it is largely as a result of the way people appear to others that they form collective identities at all. In the case of identity as home, for example, it may be an immigrant group's lack of welcome to which it is a reaction, and this may be manifest, as I said, in its members feeling themselves to be only obtrusive bodies-for-others for non-members. For members they are unobtrusive and at home, the bodily features responsible for this difference of treatment becoming markers of identity. Similar considerations apply to other types of identity. The second reason is that achieving a collective identity depends upon establishing a difference between the ways in which one appears to fellow members and to others, and this will be to a large degree a corporeal difference. This is so even when establishing this difference is not the primary point of the identity, as it is with identity as face. For it is necessary for something to count as a collective identity that those possessing it should be recognisable at least to fellow members as having it, so that the difference of non-members can be discriminated.

There are, I suggest, several parameters of difference involved as between member-to-member appearance and member-to-non-member appearance. The first is in degree of obtrusiveness to non-members compared to unobtrusiveness to members. Roughly speaking, this corresponds to how different from another somebody else appears to them. This is no simple matter, for social and political factors will mark some features as obtrusive and not others that are, in some sense, objectively equally different. Thus the taboos of one group are likely to lead to breaches of them by members of another group being discerned as markers of obtrusive difference, whether in clothing, cleanliness, bodily distance, loudness or whatever. Among many related factors, political relationships with members of another group can affect how they appear. One has only to think of the depiction of the Irish in the nineteenth century as ape-like and contrast that with their near invisibility as different today to appreciate this point. What is going on here is that certain factors are seen in accordance with one group's stereotype of another, itself formed in relation to the construction of its own identity.

A second parameter is the degree of comprehensibility of the body-for-others to non-members compared with its presumed transparency to members. This will correlate inversely, other things being equal, to its degree of obtrusiveness as different, so that it is not as the same as my own that the body of another member of my identity group is registered, but simply as 'normal', as we say – that is, regulated by the norms by which I regulate my own. With non-members I may take the trouble to learn their 'body language' just as I might acquire their spoken language. Or I might not be able to do so, either because of resistance on my own part or because, on theirs, this system of signs that provides their point of view in the world is deliberately hermetic – sealed against being understood by others to preserve a distinctive face, for example, as in the case of much behaviour with religious meanings. But it needs to be stressed again that this incomprehension is not to be thought of as a failure to penetrate through the outer to the inner. It is, rather, an inability to join in with their behaviour, to act as a member of their own group would, so that the world would take on for us a similar aspect as for them. The introduction of new dance forms from other cultures, at first alien, then enthusiastically adopted, as our own bodies learn the moves, exemplifies on a small scale what would be involved.

The third parameter of difference between member-to-member and member-to-non-member appearances of the body that I wish to mention is in affective reactions. Alien bodies can induce a variety of negative emotions not generally felt towards familiar ones – disgust, fear, detestation and so on. All of these involve bodily reactions – of recoil, agitation, scowling, and so on. The body-for-self, that is to say, develops a certain condition through which another's body is experienced as distasteful, menacing, odious or whatever. These involve, in Sartre's phrase, knowing only 'the Other-as-object'.[19] It is through these and other less extreme and less readily classifiable bodily reactions that members of one group differentiate themselves from those of another. It is not that the unlikeness of the other is discerned and then reacted against, but that this sort of bodily reaction is itself the registration of unlikeness. Or alternatively, the other may not be reacted against in this way, but simply not be reacted to positively with the movement and warmth towards them that constitutes the experience of meeting a fellow. While identity as difference conduces to the former, more dangerous, reaction, identity as home needs only the latter; and identity as centre may involve either, depending upon the sort of cultural values it instantiates. Or again, to put the same point differently, what values it instantiates depends upon such facts as how bearers of the identity are brought to react physically to non-bearers.

The three parameters of difference I have itemised are not, then, independent. How members appear to each other as bodies-for-others and how they appear to non-members are themselves dependent upon the way the bodies-for-self of those they appear to are affected. Obtrusiveness is, to some degree, a function of negative, or at least non-positive, reactions. Readability, its inverse correlate, normally presupposes a reciprocity to which such reactions are antithetical. Some of the parameters, as I have already indicated in relation to affective reactions, are more important for some types of identity. Readability by members, for another example, is crucial to identity as centre, since it presupposes a grasp of values manifest in behaviour that fellow members will possess, so that without it no common centre can be assumed. Unobtrusiveness to members, as suggested earlier, is a feature of identity as home. Examples could be multiplied, but the point I wish to stress is the complex way in which different types of cultural identity are dependent upon the availability of a range of differentiated bodily reactions which can be inculcated into their bearers.

Another way of expressing these points is to say that the cultural meanings of the bodies of fellow members of a group and of the bodies of others depend upon the types of identity round which the group is constructed, and that these meanings, in their turn, depend upon the kinds of bodily reaction those bodies elicit. In the case of the bodies of fellow members these are the meanings which the members take their bodies to have and which they are, other things being equal, comfortable to display. In the case of the bodies of non-members, however, the meanings depend upon assignments by those who react to those bodies in a different way, and one which may or may not be predicted or intended by non-members. This may itself provoke, I have suggested, a variety of reactions associated with different types of identity. None of this is simple, and none of it gives any reason for postulating some uniform kind of cultural identity, differing from case to case only in its cultural content, to which there are standard reactions and counter-reactions between members and non-members of the culture.

Surface Identity

I want to conclude, however, by questioning the significance of cultural identity, even in the multiform character we have attributed to it. It will have been evident that much of what we have said about bodily markers of cultural identity and reactions to them could equally have been said about so-called racial or ethnic identities. Markers of these identities can elicit analogous differential reactions which either parallel or transect those made in respect of cultural, for example national, identities. But then similar reactions can be provoked by members of social classes, occupational groups, age cohorts, or what are referred to as subcultural groups, such as 'Goths' or 'hippies'. There just is a highly complex pattern of social relationships of inclusion and exclusion for some purposes and not for others, of which those based on cultural identity are but a small subclass.

The difference between cultural identity and these other forms of identification lies in the sort of political claims it is invoked to justify. Other forms are principally concerned with equal treatment of one sort or another – an end to racial discrimination, equal access to health care and education for working-class citizens, and so forth. Cultural identity groups, by contrast, seek recognition of their distinctiveness through various kinds of differential treatment. In the case of identity as home what is sought may be a space within which members can engage in those practices that enable them to feel at home. For immigrants, without their own territorial space, this may involve demands for toleration of practices, not generally acceptable in the wider community, regarding dress, diet, the upbringing of children, and so on. Mme Silmi's wearing of a *burqa* may, as we saw, be among such practices. Or it may, as an expression of identity as centre, go with demands that a different legal code, at least in family law, be applied to Muslims on the grounds of their different ethical ideals. Again, examples could be multiplied. What is common to them is that recognition is taken to require political accommodation.

But recognition of distinctiveness is itself facilitated by visible difference. Even if members of a group seeking recognition normally dress indistinguishably from others those who represent them politically are often elders in traditional garb, or they are by other marks anxious to be seen to be different when advancing claims for different treatment. The embodiment of cultural identity has in this respect a political function. But political claims need, of course, the strongest possible case behind them and the case for different treatment is taken to be the stronger the deeper the differences to be recognised are taken to go. On the one hand this leads inexorably to employing the picture of deep-going cultural differences which, I have argued, a cool scrutiny of identities does not support. On the other hand it leads to an exaggeration of whatever points of difference there are, which is itself most easily expressed in emphatic visible difference. Mme Silmi's *burqa* is an example of this. For the less accommodation is made the more attention will be drawn to the differences for which it is sought, and cultural identities will be embodied in more obvious, and to others disturbing, ways.

The sort of identity that this story of embodiment reveals is what I call *surface* identity, just by contrast with the supposedly deep sort. It is an identity worn, as it were, on the surface of the body and consisting only in this, whatever deep concomitants it has in particular individuals. Surface identity is what enables someone to be picked out by others, so it may seem as if deep and surface identity conceptions are not in opposition but that the respective identities are doing different jobs: the former suggesting what it is that makes someone the person she is, the latter merely how she is to be recognised as that person. And it is no accident that deep identity conceptions seem to provide an account too of a person's sense of herself as a subject, indeed, as the particular subject that she is. Yet critiques of deep conceptions are in fact aimed at unsettling the idea that there really is something that makes one who one is of the sort that those conceptions suggest – something over and above what simply picks one out from others. For, of course, when I think of myself as a particular person, with my own desires, viewpoints or story, I am not engaged in any practical task of distinguishing myself from others, as if I could somehow go wrong about who I am, though others can make just this sort of mistake about me. Surface conceptions are, then, genuinely in competition with deep ones as providing an account of identity, since they deny that there is a viable notion of collective cultural identity as to who one is in some non-recognitional sense.

When we come to looking at collective identities, however, it becomes clear that identities under the two different kinds of conception play contrasting roles. Under the deep conception collective identities are constituted by those aspects of deep identity shared between members of the collectivity, be they values, perspectives or narratives. But there could, on the deep conception, be error as to this constitutive fact, so that all that a sufficiency of putative members actually share is a false belief about what they have in common. On a surface conception this unwelcome consequence should be averted. For here members of the group will be recognised by shared surface features and ascribed an identity thereby. Yet such a surface feature will scarcely be the sort of thing about which there could be any considerable error, as well there might be for a deep psychological one. Indeed, on this account the whole point of a group designating what is in fact a surface feature as conferring collective identity will be to ensure mutual recognition among group members, and, we should add, exclusion of non-members. It serves, so to say, as a badge of identity. For groups picked out by features of physical appearance – like skin colour – there cannot be, except at the margins, any error at all. For those where some behavioural features are criterial there could be a risk of dissimulation, but only up to that point beyond which talking the talk and walking the walk really do confer identity. Here it does not matter what, if anything, lies behind the lifestyle so long as it is practised consistently and spontaneously. All that is needed for this, I suggest, is that it is found tolerably comfortable and attractive.

A common way of life, then, often thought to be what marks out a culture, can be regarded as a purely surface feature if we discount any supposed psychological under-pinnings for it. Then a cultural identity, by this criterion, would be a surface identity. All that is needed for someone to have it is that they practise overtly the way of life that is shared with fellow members of the culture and that is distinct in recognisable ways from that of other cultures. If there are to be cultural identities in this sense then there must be such recognisable ways of life. They will be pos-sessed by groups which have a sense of their members as collected together by their sharing a distinctive way of life. Of course it is quite possible that this may be accompanied by beliefs in a deeper identity, but these, whether true or false, are unnecessary, so long as the relevant surface features of the way of life are grasped by members, explicitly or implicitly, in how members are distinguished from non-members. Then mentioning someone's cultural identity explains a bit of their behaviour by fitting it into this overt pattern of activity which characterises the group's lifestyle and that is all: no psychological explanations are required.

All this may seem hopelessly reductive. For it seems to ignore the fact that the bits of behaviour we are thus explaining have meaning for their agents and they do so in virtue of expressing what Charles Taylor calls a shared 'social imaginary'.[20] Thus let us return to the Islamic concept of purity, which is intricately bound up with practices of ablution and purification. Conversely, the practices have the significance they do only because of their relation to the concept. And, of course, this concept is tied in to a system including ideas of bodily gratification and sin contrasting with self-control and the journey to Allah. Here, we might say, is a social imaginary collecting Muslims together and distinguishing them from non-believers as a different sort of people. And we might say this not because of their distinctive values, though values are intimately involved in their imaginary, but because of the sort of subjects they have been constituted as through the language of the Koran and the practices of Islam.

Islam claims, it is said, a kind of monopoly over the thoughts and actions of its adherents; but it is implausible to suppose that it could ever be completely successful in achieving such a monopoly. Muslims, like everyone else, will, to use our current apparatus, have access to a mixture of social imaginaries corresponding to the different languages and practices they have mastered and employ. But can we not speak of an Islamic cultural identity as what is common to Muslims on account of their having this identity; and *pari passu* for other cultural groups? On the face of it, religious groups with sacred texts providing a language for believers look like a comparatively easy case for delimiting what we are to call a culture here, and hence a cultural identity. Yet even this appearance is deceptive. For the same religion with the same texts and practices can play a very different role in people's lives in different times and places. It is precisely the attempt to impose uniformity on this variety that constitutes contemporary Islamism. Until it succeeds we may safely say that there are many different sorts of Muslim; and similarly for any other alleged cultural identity. All we so far have here is, at best, a surface identity. For what are seemingly shared are religious language use and practice.

This response may well seem unsatisfying. Part of the point of speaking of an imaginary associated with a culture here is to make sense, as Taylor puts it, of the common behaviour of members of a culture. This, we may say, is to show how the way they experience things gives them a reason for acting as they do. It is the involvement of experience that apparently gives psychological depth to the identity of those who do so act. Then surely, it will be objected, despite the variety of ways in which people can be Muslims, or members of any other cultural group picked out in terms of its social imaginary, their common practices must be explained by reference to common experiences. And in that case they share a deep cultural identity.

Several points need making here. The first is that common practices need not be explained by common experiences because they need not be explained by any experience at all. Modern Western town dwellers lock their doors on leaving home, while inhabitants of remote rural communities perhaps still do not. But the former do not typically have some experience of the insecurity and vulnerability of their possessions before turning the key, and may leave their homes with feelings no different from the latter's. Similarly, there is no reason to think that Muslims bathe after sexual intercourse because it makes them feel dirty. They may have no relevant experience of it at all. Furthermore, where an experience is identifiable as an individual's reason for engaging in a culturally shared practice there may be no uniformity in such experiences between members of the culture even when an imaginary is shared. While one person leaving home may experience her meagre possessions as exposed and vulnerable, another may lock his door with satisfaction on his treasure house of enviable acquisitions: both act in the same way. A snorting bull may fill the nervous with apprehension, while this sign of its virility thrills the farmer: both treat it with the same respect. In other societies, bulls occupying a different place in their social imaginary are treated differently. There is so much room for individual variation in the salience that things have for us that it would be wrong to postulate shared experiences as explaining common practice, even where a social imaginary is shared. Some Muslims may feel dirty after sex; others may just feel hot and sweaty, but their bathing does not lose its religious significance because of this.

I want to infer, not unexpectedly, that shared social practice yields only a surface collective identity however deep going someone's individual reasons for engaging in it may be. What is recognisably the same is the way people act, given the language or other representational system they all use. Talk of a common social imaginary here is potentially misleading if taken to imply something inner that they share as well. But all that it should imply is a common grasp of concepts manifest in, where appropriate, a common way of acting through the use of them. Yet even this, I have suggested, should make us cautious about ascribing shared cultural identities, if only surface ones, in view of the variety of languages, broadly conceived, and their related imaginaries that are in play for any individual. The way people identify a shared cultural identity amid this complexity is due to other – and, as I have argued, political – factors.

Notes

1. As at the time of writing; see Robert O. Paxton, 'Can you really become French?', *The New York Review of Books*, LVI.6 (9–29 April 2009), pp. 52–6.
2. Ibid. p. 53.
3. *The Quran*, 4:35.
4. For example, Matthew Festenstein, *Negotiating Diversity* (Cambridge: Polity, 2005), ch. 1.
5. See for example, S. Burwood, P. Gilbert and K. Lennon, *Philosophy of Mind* (London: University College London Press, 1999), ch. 1.
6. Jean Paul Sartre, *Being and Nothingness*, trans. H. E. Barnes (London: Methuen, 1969), p. 305.
7. Ibid. pp. 323, 328, 329, 332.
8. Ibid. p. 328.
9. Ibid. p. 349.
10. Ibid. p. 344.
11. Ibid. pp. 351, 353.
12. M. Merleau-Ponty, *Phenomenology of Perception*, trans. C. Smith (London: Routledge, 1965), p. 361.
13. Ibid. p. 353.
14. Ibid. p. 106, fn. 1.
15. Ibid. p. 189. In fact, smiling is not an expression of anger for the Japanese but a conventional way of hiding emotions.
16. See for example, Festenstein, *Negotiating Diversity*.
17. al-Qaradawi, quoted in Malise Ruthven, *Islam: a Very Short Introduction* (Oxford: Oxford University Press, 1997), p. 108.
18. Judith Butler, 'Variations on sex and gender: Beauvoir, Wittig and Foucault', in P. Rice and P. Waugh (eds), *Modern Literary Theory: a Reader* (London: Arnold, 1996).
19. Sartre, *Being and Nothingness*, p. 411.
20. Charles Taylor, *Modern Social Imaginaries* (Durham, NC: Duke University Press, 2004), ch. 2.

6
Identity and Subjectivity

Freud on Identity

An immediate objection to the account I have offered of cultural identities as merely surface phenomena is that it neglects the way in which they are internalised by their subjects, so that it flies in the face of, for example, psychoanalytic accounts of identity. Psychoanalysis, it has been suggested, 'could be described as a theory of unhappy relationships'.[1] What unhappier relationships are there, one might ask, than those that so often exist between members of different national, ethnic, religious, or other identity groups? What relationships are there, at least, that give rise to so much unhappiness and misery? Can we, then, look to psychoanalysis for a theory of such relationships – a theory that explains their unhappy character and, it might be hoped, shows us a way of overcoming it?

For psychoanalysis, of course, is not only a theory, it is a therapy – a therapy designed to reduce unhappiness, or, at least, the adverse effects of the patient's condition on him- or herself and others. This aim constitutes, I take it, 'the ethics of psychoanalysis' to which Julia Kristeva refers. 'The ethics of psychoanalysis implies a politics,'[2] she maintains, precisely because psychoanalysis can explain the conflictual relationships between members of different national and cultural groups, since it is in politics that these relationships are institutionalised and therefore in politics that their adverse consequences can be alleviated – or exacerbated. I shall return to Kristeva's own account in due course. But my present aim is to explore more generally the scope for psychoanalytic accounts of national and cultural identities – to ask what they explain and how they explain it, to assess their plausibility, and to enquire into the contribution they might make to conflict resolution. In particular, we must address the question of whether cultural identities, whatever their character, are somehow a necessary consequence of human psychology and what repercussions such a claim would have for politics.

Sigmund Freud was, of course, the first to offer a psychoanalytic account of national and similar identities, though, in fact, within a wider project of group psychology. But Freud himself derives his account not only from his general theory of psychoanalysis but from his reflections upon earlier thinkers about group formation and behaviour, like Gustave Le Bon and Wilfrid Trotter. The late nineteenth-century French thinker Le Bon appealed to Freud since he believed that most group behaviour is the result of unconscious processes rather than the conscious deliberations of individual members. Thus he thought that groups, like nations, once formed were hard to change by educative methods. For 'it is not the living but the dead who play the preponderating role in the existence of a people. They are the creators of its morality and the unconscious sources of its conduct.'[3] People are bound together into a group and act according to its mores, then, because they unconsciously conform to a common pattern laid down by their predecessors.

Wilfred Trotter wrote at the start of the First World War, a spectacle of mass destruction that was to have a considerable influence on Freud. Trotter saw the war as triggering the 'gregarious instinct' of members of the opposing nations, utilising a concept he had borrowed from the social psychologist William McDougall. Like him, Trotter viewed this instinct as naturally producing a certain sort of homogeneity in the group as a result of our innate desire to be surrounded by others who share their emotional reactions. 'From homogeneity,' writes Trotter, 'proceed moral power, enthusiasm, courage, endurance, enterprise, and all the virtues of the warrior.'[4] Trotter, however, discerns three types of 'herd instinct', 'the aggressive, the protective, and the socialised, which are exemplified in Nature by the wolf, the sheep, and the bee respectively'. While England manifested the 'spirit of the hive', he maintains, German aggression was due to 'a reappearance of the society of the wolf'[5] – a diagnosis that Freud regretted as reflecting 'the antipathies loosened by the recent great war'.[6]

While Freud shared with McDougall and his followers the view that instincts provide the drive for behaviour, he rejects the notion of a separate herd instinct as lacking in explanatory power: there is no independent evidence for the instinct but the behaviour it is postulated to explain. Instead, Freud aims to account for the kind of group phenomenon observed by Le Bon and Trotter in terms of processes of individual psychology which have quite other manifestations. In particular, he takes from McDougall and Trotter the idea that groups are held together by emotional bonds involving identification, and from Le Bon an appreciation of the very different foci of their identifications and of the hostilities these differences can engender. But, rather than regarding these as processes that essentially require the existence of suitable collectivities, Freud explains them as, so to speak, large-scale realisations of the forms of small-scale relationships, originally infantile ones, in whose study psychoanalysis originates.

In group formation two individual processes observed in everyday personal relationships are, according to Freud, discernible. In the first process, narcissistic feelings are involved, as the subject seeks to identify with the one he loves, and loves him because of the perceived likeness. The object of love provides what Freud terms an 'ego-ideal' on which the subject models his behaviour, and which is 'introjected' into the self in such a way as to expand the range of what he finds desirable. This process, originating in a child's relationship with a parent (in particular, Freud believed, one of the same sex), continues later in the formation of certain sorts of love relationship; and it is thus to love relationships, with their types of emotional charge, that Freud looks for a model of the ties within a group.

What binds members together, Freud claims, is that they 'have put one and the same object in the place of their ego ideal and have consequently identified with one another in their ego'.[7] The ego ideal may be provided by a leader, a figure of the past or some less concrete object of emulation. Members of the group are in the first place, then, united by their sharing of such an ideal, but also through their recognition of this similarity, so that they identify not only with the ideal but with each other. These ties are libidinal ones because they are driven by 'love instincts which have been diverted from their original aims' (i.e. sex),[8] and since these are aim-inhibited, without a definite goal to achieve or fail to achieve, the ties they form are potentially long lasting ones. What Freud offers here is a general account of how group identities are constituted by individual processes which have a common focus. What is less clear is why there are these common foci which is, perhaps, what McDougall's gregarious instinct was designed to explain.

This, then, is the first process involved in group formation, according to Freud, and it may, indeed, be sufficient in itself. But Freud links it to a second process which involves not just libidinal instinct but the 'death-drive', which he postulated as necessary to explain the sort of events witnessed in the First World War. Though he had, of course, previously recognised the existence of aggression, it was only after his association of it with a separate drive that it came to play an explanatory role in accounting for behaviour. Aggressive feelings, Freud believes, are projected upon others as their objects in order to rationalise their occurrence as they arise naturally in any relationship, competing with feelings of love. In group formation, however, these feelings are directed against non-members so that members are related solely by libidinous impulses. In setting up an ego-ideal, Freud observes, 'the subject behaves as though any divergence from his own particular lines of development involved a criticism',[9] and it is accordingly aggressively resisted. In the group case, the differences of those outside the group – however minor – attract an aggressive response which further serves to focus members upon those characteristics which differentiate them from others. This phenomenon exemplifies Freud's theory of the narcissism of minor differences, which can be used to explain group loyalties and antagonisms.

So far, Freud's account applies to any group and to any individual identity constituted by group membership. But Freud draws upon it specifically to deal with national and cultural groups. People's satisfaction in belonging to such groups is narcissistic, resting upon pride in what the group has achieved in establishing certain ideals. Freud writes,

> To make this satisfaction complete calls for a comparison with other cultures which have . . . developed different ideals. On the strength of these differences every culture claims the right to look down on the rest. In this way cultural ideals become a source of discord and enmity between different cultural units, as can be seen most clearly in the case of nations.[10]

Here Freud adapts Le Bon's account of the origins of cultural norms to his own theory of ego ideals, and McDougall's and Trotter's account of group identification to his theory of aggression. In the case of national and cultural groups, then, cultural ideals play their part both in the first process of group formation discussed above, and in the second, both unifying group members and separating them antagonistically from non-members.

What sort of politics does Freud's account imply? On the face of it, it does seem to imply that, insofar as nations and other cultural groups are a primary focus of group loyalty, then this is a fact which, as theorists like David Miller[11] – following Le Bon – have agreed, must simply be accommodated within politics: it is not something that people can be argued or educated out of, at least in the short term. It may also imply that it is dangerous to erode cultural differences. For, as John McGarry and Brendan O'Leary, writing on Northern Ireland, express Freud's theory of the narcissism of minor differences: 'the more cultural differences there are, the deeper they are, then the greater the likelihood that collective identities will be secure rather than threatened'.[12] And we may expect a threat to identity to meet with resistance, possibly violent, under this theory. Yet Freud's account of groups is, as I said, quite general. There is no necessity that political groupings should be organised around the kind of ideals usually thought of as cultural, in that they encompass a wide range of life activities rather than just political ones. Thus it is not clear that cultural groups cannot remain secure within a framework of more narrowly political ones in which antagonisms can be managed pacifically. The way to do this, if Freud is right, is to substitute for existing divergent ego ideals a single more inclusive one, though this will generate new risks of fresh conflicts. But it does illustrate the malleability of collective identity and thus unsettles the picture of deep identity which Freud's account initially seems to support. There is, however, nothing in it to count against this malleability which is exemplified in innumerable political situations.

Analysing Ulster

Let us return to the question of the role of aggression towards an out-group in maintaining the cohesiveness of an ethnic group. This question has been interestingly tackled by another writer on Northern Ireland, John Cash, in a book that might have been not inaccurately entitled 'The Ulster Defence Mechanism'.[13] What Cash aims to throw light on is 'the persistence and resurgence of ideologies of ethnicity', and he does so by rejecting both pluralist explanations, in terms of the continuity of primordial ethnic identities, and modernisation accounts, which sharply contrast the rational pursuit of group interest with irrational prejudices. Instead, Cash emphasises the fluctuations in ideology – most especially the Ulster Unionist one – in relation to changing political circumstances. He conceives of the individuals who occupy positions within the social order constructed by an ideology in psychoanalytic terms – in particular those of Kleinian rather than Freudian theory. Such individuals are 'capable of "rational" calculation, but always subject to paranoid and depressive anxieties and the defensive formations which attend these',[14] and these anxieties will arise in response to threats to the group, impairing the capacity to make a rational response to such threats.

Cash draws upon Melanie Klein's account of infant development, in which the child's experience of the breast veers between satisfaction and frustration, giving rise to idealisation of the good breast and aggression against the bad. This so-called paranoid-schizoid position is one to which the adult can regress whenever he *splits* the world into good and bad objects, rather than objects with good and bad aspects. This, Cash suggests, occurs in intergroup relationships which are conceived in terms of an interaction between good and evil, like those that affect Unionists and Nationalists under certain political circumstances; and he illustrates the point by textual analysis of Unionist ideology at different periods of the Troubles, which he sees as dehumanising or persecutory. It is a defence mechanism resorted to in order to reduce anxiety, but not only does it distort the reality of the situation, it also exacerbates group conflict.

Cash combines this psychodynamic account with aspects of Kohlberg's cognitive-developmental theory to devise rules governing the structuration of identities and relations in Northern Ireland. He discerns four modes of ideological reasoning: two corporate ones which constitute persons by their ethno-religious category, the instrumental through shared objectives and the affiliative through allegiance; and two liberal ones, the conventional which constitutes them as citizens and the post-conventional as human beings. The suitability of the corporate modes to the dehumanising or persecutory positions, and of the liberal to a more ambivalent one, is evident. Terms like 'Protestant' and 'Roman Catholic' thus have a different significance depending on whether the corporate or liberal modes are employed, and these involve either exclusivist or inclusivist constructions of the social world respectively. This is the basis of Cash's 'depth hermeneutic of Unionist ideology'.[15] In speeches by Unionist politicians he identifies the changes from liberal ambivalence to corporate dehumanisation or persecutory anxiety and back again.

If the strength of Cash's theory of ideology is to be judged by its power to explain Unionist politics then it cannot be judged a complete success. His somewhat one-dimensional account does not take us far beyond recording the readily observable affective reactions of Unionists to political events. Though he dwells on the paradox of a Loyalism which defies British authority and asserts a right of self-government, his scheme fails to elucidate what Britishness means to Unionists. Nor does his downplaying of their Protestantism as just a potentially exclusionary label help capture their complex identity. But it is, I suppose, his reluctance to look outside his confiningly *pathological* framework that is finally unsatisfying: Nationalists are described as exclusivist when, for them, 'the enemy was trying to continue with its regime of oppression and discrimination'.[16] But it was, wasn't it?

Whatever one makes of Cash's application of this theory to Northern Ireland, it does potentially have several advantages over Freud's. First, the Kleinian theory, whatever its official stance, does not treat aggression as a biological given, but rather as an intelligible response to frustration – a much more plausible account. Second, and consequentially, aggression does not need to be thought of as an invariable ingredient of group formation. Rather it is a feature of groups under particular sorts of pressure. Third, therefore, it implies a rather different politics from Freud's theory – not a politics of accommodation and control, but rather of reassurance and removal of threats to group identity, the result of which should, paradoxically, be a reduction of polarisation, as well as of conflict.

Here, then, are two psychoanalytic theories with somewhat divergent prescriptions, though it is beyond our scope to adjudicate between them. But, they have in common a feature which might make us doubt the utility of either in yielding a political solution to the problems of nationalism and ethnic conflict. It is that both betray what Jürgen Habermas describes as a 'scientific self-misunderstanding' of psychoanalysis, viewing it as an observational science rather than as an unequivocally hermeneutic enterprise which 'initiates the appropriation of a lost portion of a life'.[17] Yet it is, arguably, only if psychoanalysis functions in this latter, interpretive way that it can motivate a genuine politics. For political actors need to come to see their situation in the terms that psychoanalysis discloses but that were previously hidden to them. Only then will they be able to *accept* something as a political solution to their problems. Yet they will not be able to come to such a realisation if they think of themselves simply as in the grip of psycho-dynamical forces, rather than coming to grasp the *reasons* for their affective reactions which were previously obscure to them. At best, a psychoanalytic explanation conceived in the former scientistic way could be used to manipulate people; but it could not be used to bring people to see their situation differently and effect political change accordingly.

'We are all Foreigners'

Freud's naturalistic conception of the unconscious as an arena of psychodynamical forces was rejected by Jacques Lacan who holds instead that 'the unconscious is structured like a language'[18] and therefore that identity is a social product. Lacan develops his own story of how a child comes to conceive of herself as a being with a separate identity. In the first place, the subject lacks any prior identity: the identity she gains has to be established by a process of identification. Second, the individual gains her identity only by contrast with that of the other, who is, in the first instance, normally the mother. In the drawing of this contrast, furthermore, negative emotions of hostility and jealousy towards the other are implicated. Third, however, in Hegelian vein, the dependence of the individual's identity upon this contrast – this alterity within the self, as it is metaphorically expressed – implies a lack of self-sufficiency, stability and security in identity. The maintenance of identity is therefore a process perpetually focused upon uneasy transactions with those who are other than oneself. Next, recognition of identity involves identification with *images* of the self – in the first instance, on Lacan's account, with one's mirror image, although this is not necessarily to be understood literally. This process is bound up with positive emotions of a narcissistic character as well as aggressive ones. Lastly, this self-identification involves taking up a subject position in a pre-existing system of relationships, in the early stages, family ones including the figure of the father. This constitutes an entry into the symbolic order, for identity is fully gained only through acquiring the language within which it is constituted.

Julia Kristeva draws upon several features of Lacan's story of identity formation in her account of national and ethnic identities, though she introduces another process into the chronology represented by Lacan's mirror stage and entry into the symbolic order. Lacan sees the mirror stage as the time when the child first breaks out of its original experience of unity with the mother and begins to establish an independent identity. Kristeva, however, regards this as only a secondary repression. The primary repression consists in what Kristeva terms *abjection* – the throwing out of a part of the self, whose physical manifestation is the spitting out of the mother's milk. It is this act of abjection, constantly repeated in other forms, which Kristeva sees as necessary to maintain the boundaries of the self and to prevent it being swamped in what is beyond it.

In her book, *Powers of Horror*,[19] Kristeva provides a phenomenological account of experiences arising from confrontation with what has been abjected. These are characterised by a variety of emotions marked by simultaneous attraction and revulsion, most notably in our reactions to what is *uncanny*. Here Kristeva draws on and develops Freud's own investigations in his essay on 'The "Uncanny"'[20] – *Das Unheimliche*. Here Freud himself characterises the impression of uneasiness as due to 'a regression to a time when the ego had not yet marked itself off sharply from the external world and from other people',[21] and this explains why 'the uncanny [*unheimliche*] is something which is secretly familiar [*heimlich-heimisch*], which has undergone repression and then returned to it'.[22] Elsewhere Freud characterises the unconscious as 'internal foreign territory'.[23] What is important for our present purposes is that Kristeva discerns the experience of uncanny strangeness in confrontations with the foreigner. For what I abject in establishing a social identity is that which characterises those I count as strangers. But since this is, prior to abjection, a part of me and, at the level of the unconscious remains so, 'the foreigner is,' as Kristeva puts it, 'within me hence we are all foreigners'.[24] That is why, she goes on, 'the ethics of psychoanalysis implies a politics', and it is to her account of this aspect that we now turn.

The first point to make about Kristeva's account is that it is specifically about the identity acquired through membership of those groups non-members of which are experienced as *foreigners*. It is not, like Freud's, a general account of group psychology, but of the psychology of – in the modern world – *national* and *ethnic* groups. Kristeva's criterion for applying her abjection account seems, then, to be a phenomenological one – that it is just these groups which elicit the reaction that is to be so explained. Why this should be is not a question she takes up. But that it is so reveals that what is involved in such group formations is not simply the marking of boundaries in the symbolic order. The affective reactions which are associated with these boundaries reveal that they have become linked with the primary repression that establishes the subject as an independent agent at all. As such they are present in the realm of what Kristeva calls the *semiotic* – the pre-symbolic. There is a sense, then, in which what really differentiates one from the foreigner is something which eludes expression.

This is what explains the indeterminacy and ambivalence of the response the foreigner provokes. It is anxiety rather than any specific fear, both disturbance *and* fascination. This ambivalence is aptly illustrated by the example of gypsies, who are simultaneously vilified and romanticised. The example also serves to indicate how the boundaries of the group are maintained through harnessing reactions which are, nonetheless, themselves unstable and unreliable, so that there can be no security in membership. To go, perhaps, a little beyond Kristeva herself, there can be *in principle* no removal of the threat to group cohesiveness, which, for thinkers like John Cash, is necessary to curb the reactions of exclusiveness and aggression. For the threat is ever present of the individual losing those features which integrate her as an agent and which she shares with others through a common pattern of socialisation.

The response to this threat should, however, Kristeva argues, be to acknowledge the presence within one, albeit repressed, of those features which the foreigner has retained rather than, like me, abjected. This is the sense in which 'we are all foreigners'. It is this fact which makes it possible, she thinks, to put oneself in the foreigner's place and to imagine living as he does – something which would not be possible if his motivations were entirely alien to ours. This is, furthermore, the attitude we should take up if we respond appropriately to the phenomenology of our reaction to foreigners. It is the attitude which the self-understanding of acknowledging the foreigner within will lead us to adopt, and it is, of course, an attitude with large political consequences – in particular, of an acceptance and tolerance of difference which does not depend upon a culturally located liberal creed. Yet, Kristeva insists, this acceptance does not imply an erosion of difference. Although 'if I am a foreigner, there are no foreigners',[25] still 'we cannot suppress the symptom that the foreigner provokes'.[26] To suppose otherwise would be to deny that our collective identities are tied to the inevitable processes of abjection. This makes cosmopolitanism of the classical variety impossible, and contrasts Kristeva's position sharply with, for example, that of Habermas. 'Can the "foreigner",' asks Kristeva at the beginning of *Strangers to Ourselves*, 'disappear from modern societies?'[27] concluding, it would seem, that he cannot.

However, Kristeva's own position is not a pessimistic one. It does allow for the possibility of genuine political change rather than mere accommodation. In particular, she thinks that a characteristically French republicanism can be refashioned to allow for the greater cultural diversity which French citizens themselves can come to accept. But this is specifically a vision for France, with its particular cultural resources. Elsewhere, Kristeva recognises that the dangers of national and ethnic identification need to be addressed differently. 'The exclusion of "others",' she writes, 'which binds the identity of a clan, a sect, a party or a nation is equally the source of the pleasure of identification . . . and of barbaric persecution.'[28] The trigger, Kristeva notes, for these 'aggressive, paranoid excesses' is *shame*, induced by 'underestimating, or degrading a narcissistic image or ego ideal'[29] from which a group derives its national pride. Kristeva's model of identity is, then, what we earlier termed identity as standing, which, for Freudian reasons, she takes to underlie all cultural identities. Kristeva is, however, apprehensive of entrenching forms of identification, for example, ethnic ones, which would stand in the way of accepting cultural diversity within political units, which would stand in the way, in other words, of acknowledging that 'the foreigner is within me'. The reason such identities stand in the way of this is that they leave little room for choice and change. But Kristeva wants *political* membership to be subject to choice, to 'clarity of vision', rather than 'a reflex or return to origin', as she puts it.[30] For once we grasp that our reactions to others, especially those that disparage or degrade them, are founded on abjection then, though 'we cannot repress the symptoms', we shall see that they provide no reason for political affiliations.

We may conclude by drawing out some implications of this last point. Many contemporary theorists of nationalism, like David Miller, treat national identification as a given, and use this fact to construct arguments, however qualified, for conceding political recognition to national groups. The advantage, as I see it, of psychoanalytic accounts is that they look behind what is supposedly given to investigate the processes involved in such identifications. If, like Kristeva's, these accounts are ones that can bring individuals to see their actions and attitudes in a new light then they call into question whether these identifications should be regarded as simply given, so far as politics is concerned. For, however basic the cultural reactions we acquire in early socialisation are, there seems to be no reason why such shared reactions should require a common political organisation. The idea of the nation, however, is an inherently political one: a nation is, to put it loosely, a group of a sort with a claim to separate statehood. In the same way, the notion of cultural identity is employed to claim certain kinds of political recognition: without this, cultural affinities are not usually marked as identity. There is, though, no reason why our reactions to others as foreign or culturally different should be marshalled, as they are in the modern world, along national or cultural lines – rather than, say, along local ones for which no political significance is sought. And where they are marshalled along national lines, say, we need to ask in whose interests they are – interests which, when brought to light, may rightly influence people's political choices. What is claimed as cultural identity has a political rather than a psychological explanation.

Ideology and Identity

'The working men have no country,'[31] wrote Marx and Engels, famously denying, in effect, that their national identity is of any deep significance to them in determining how they should think of themselves and how they should act. In any case, they go on, national differences are disappearing through the development of world markets. The result is that national and other cultural identities are, in a certain sense, illusory in that they misrepresent what are real facts about people's interests and relationships in terms that obscure and distort them. Language is, Marx and Engels, would acknowledge, a real tie, but that is evidently for them just because it facilitates communication; and they have little time for the political claims of linguistic minorities when these stand in the way of the extended scope of social relations required by the modern state. While these minorities have been oppressed, the reaction represented by their separatist political claims is wrongly focused, as a result, in part, of liberal conceptualisations of their situation which perpetuate the illusions about themselves under which they labour.

This account is, of course, dependent upon the Marxian theory of ideology – the system of ideas in terms of which people conceptualise their social lives, but which, rather than reflecting the reality it describes, is determined by features of those lives and, in particular, by the power relations which they involve, so that the dominant ideology will serve the interests of the most powerful. The first aspect of this theory, that ideology induces a 'false consciousness', is no longer fashionable. In relation to Marx's attack on the reality of national and other cultural identities, for example, it might be objected that this presupposes the existence of a real identity which such illusory identities conceal, with dire consequences for thought and action. It is indeed true that Marx, especially in his earlier work, does sometimes talk in a way that might suggest this, positing a 'species being', from which people have become alienated under capitalism and which, to be discovered, requires not just an act of identification but a change in social relations. Yet this is precisely not to contrast an existing authentic identity with an illusory one. Indeed, Marx's notion that what people are coincides with what they do in a system of socio-economic relations can be read as a denial of identity as something underlying the way they act.

The significance of this denial, in relation to national identity especially, should not be overlooked, as the pervasiveness of ideas of national character at the time will underline. While Marx and Engels both lamentably fell into derogatory national stereotyping, the whole tenor of their theory should have restrained them. It implies that this discourse is an ideological construction which fails to reveal any differences of deep significance. So when it comes to questions of national self-determination the fundamental criterion of whether to support it is whether it will further working-class interests, for example by freeing ordinary people from particular cases of oppression. It has nothing to do with supposed rights of self-determination based upon distinctive cultural identities. It is true that this criterion may conflict with a view of social progress which condemns 'non-historical' nations to extinction, inherited from Hegel and deeply unattractive. But, overall, the Marxian attitude to national identity is not, I suggest, the matter for apology that it is often taken to be.

The second aspect of the Marxian theory of ideology as applied to national identity has been widely adopted. The idea that nationalism, with its concomitant conception of the nation as having a right to statehood, is an ideological formation that serves specific interests in particular circumstances and is unintelligible outside them – this idea has formed a leitmotiv in most contemporary thinking about the subject. Ernest Gellner's seminal thesis that 'it is nationalism which engenders nations, and not the other way round' exemplifies this. For, while Gellner goes on to deny that nationalism is 'a contingent, artificial, ideological invention',[32] this is not to deny that it is, in Marx's sense, an ideology: Gellner views nationalism as a political principle which allows a dominant class in an industrial society to impose its elite culture across it, obliterating local variations, in order to bring about the standardisation which such a society requires. Thus are nations invented, in the achievement of fit between political and cultural units. Although the empirical details of Gellner's theory have been exposed to a great deal of criticism it is essentially, in form, a view of the nation as an ideological construct serving the interests of the powerful, and this aspect has not been widely challenged.

What has been challenged is the apparent implication of 'false consciousness' in the idea of nations as invented. For, though Gellner derides Marx's 'Wrong Address Theory' – in which a call to collective consciousness, which should have been delivered to classes, in fact went to nations – yet he still presents the nationalist message as a false one, asserting the existence of cultural unity and its concomitant communal ties, when these are, at most, the effects of a uniform education system. Benedict Anderson criticises this assimilation, as he sees it, of 'invention' to 'falsification' and 'falsity', rather than 'imagining' and 'creation',[33] and with it the view of nations as ideological constructs rather than as features of a historically located cultural system. Yet the fact that his contrast is with 'self-consciously held political ideologies'[34] indicates that he fails to grasp that, for Marx, an ideology need not be self-conscious and is precisely manifest in a cultural system. Its 'falsity' – its failure to represent things as they are – does not depend, for example, as Anderson supposes, on the nation not being in some sense a real community, but on the fact that the ties that bind its members are not what they take them to be, and are such that, if they come to see their true nature and origin, they would probably reject them. It is in this way that their ideologically acquired identities fail to correspond to any deep-going facts about them.

But, someone might protest, what are these deep-going facts to which cultural identities fail to correspond? One answer is that, in the sense in which the questioner evidently conceives them, there are none. This, indeed, is the answer Louis Althusser offers in his reworking of the Marxist theory of ideology. Althusser sees ideology as relating individuals to their real conditions in an imaginary way, but a key feature of the illusion is that one has a coherent inner self from which one's actions proceed. The task of ideology is to constitute subjects as individuals labouring under this illusion. The process is achieved by, among other things, *'cramming* every citizen with daily doses of nationalism, chauvinism, liberalism, moralism etc'[35] through the mass media, as well as through early education. The real facts about us are, Althusser believes in classic Marxist fashion, only scientific ones, amongst which he numbers the psycho-analytic story of human beings as essentially fractured and incoherent. Yet this is by no means an essential part of his story of the constitution of subjectivity. The necessary illusion generated by ideology may just be that we *are* subjects of thought and action as conceived at least since Descartes, with our individual identities playing a part in a metaphysical account of human agency. For Althusser's view of how this account identifies a subject seems to be in terms of the perspective it provides on a world formed by ideology.

In fact, Althusser offers an alternative. Our identities are just what we are assigned in a process of 'interpellation',[36] in which we are, so to speak, called forth in society to act in certain regular ways. This deconstructive move is a strictly philosophical one. Viewed simply as a sceptical move against the traditional conception of the self, which shifts the onus of proof on to that conception's defenders by explaining its prevalence otherwise than by its recommendability to reason, Althusser's position avoids many of the criticisms which might be levelled against it. It does not have the intolerable consequence that we are unable to think of ourselves as subjects at all. But it takes a linguistic turn by explicating what it is to think of oneself as a subject in terms of one's using the pronoun 'I' in the appropriate way. Interpellation assigns an identity to the user of the pronoun which is dependent upon the circumstances and to whose demands he is answerable. Having an identity involves, in this sense, an identification with what is expected of one from time to time. But there is no reason to conceive this as going any deeper than behaving in the way required by the assumption of a certain identity, so that explanation of this behaviour involves revealing these regularities, not referring to any 'authentic' self with which the agent of well-schooled behaviour might sometimes be contrasted. That is why the objection that Althusser already presupposes a subject to make the necessary identifications which, for him, constitute being a subject goes astray. Identification consists only in responding to an identity's demands in a first-personal way, not in any prior metaphysical subject accepting them as its own. This is precisely the picture Althusser rejects.

Althusser's theory is a radical one, since it aims to account for subjectivity in general (at least under capitalism), not just for subjectivity as it is expressed in the identifications with the cultural formations which we have been considering and which exemplify the kind of identifications that Marx regards as ideological. Yet, if we were to restrict the scope of Althusser's critique to just such cases, it offers an instructive alternative to the deep accounts, metaphysical or supposedly empirical, which we have looked at and rejected. However, for all that, it fails to capture whatever it is that explains the *attraction* of cultural identification, adopting, as it does, the resolutely external stance of the supposedly scientific observer. But it is, perhaps, precisely the opposing stance which aims to relive the point of view of the subject that tempts one to adopt the traditional conception with its picture of inner depths that incorporate valued identities. Is there a way of recapturing the participant's point of view without adopting this model – a way that will throw light on the notion of cultural identity that both refuses it the importance for people that metaphysical and empirical accounts ascribe it and yet brings out its attractiveness to them?

Dispositions and Performances

A possible place to look for such an account is in Pierre Bourdieu's description of what he terms the *habitus* – the system of behavioural dispositions which enable us to act in the world in ways appropriate, in some sense, to it, without presupposing any conscious purposes or a grasp of how to attain them. Bourdieu uses the notion principally to distinguish the sorts of disposition that distinguish those who occupy one kind of position in the class structure from those who occupy another. However, since he thinks of their habitus as constitutive of their identity there seems no reason why his account should not be adapted to provide an account of cultural identity and its formation. Then the habitus specific to distinct cultural groups – on the large assumption that these exist and are so distinguished – would shape their members' identities. Their members would behave differently as members of different social classes typically do, as a result of divergent patterns of socialisation with differences transmitted, to some degree, across the generations.

Several features of the notion of habitus should be noted. To start with it is embodied, in the sense that it shows in the way people move and conduct themselves, the way they look and sound, and so on. All this is socially transmitted as, in the Aristotelian term, 'hexis', so that

> children are particularly attentive to the gestures and postures . . . a way of walking, a tilt of the head, facial expressions, ways of sitting and using implements . . . bodily *hexis* is a political mythology realised, *embodied*, turned into a permanent disposition, a durable manner of standing, speaking.[37]

As such, habitus is not to be thought of as a system of internalised rules or norms. No such rules could be adequately formulated, for the kinds of capacity in which habitus consists are prior to the following of rules, comprising, in large part, bodily skills which we pick up mimetically. Yet this is also to learn a right, as against a wrong, way of moving and acting. It is this sense of something being right, even though inarticulable, which those inside a set of practices may possess and those outside it, with a different habitus, will lack. In that case, 'habitus which have been produced by different modes of generation . . . cause one group to experience as natural or reasonable practices which another group find unthinkable or scandalous, and vice versa.'[38] Bourdieu illustrates these sorts of conflict with examples of aesthetic taste, which differs between those holding different positions in the class system – a system which he sees, in fact, as partly constituted by the distribution not only of economic capital but of what he terms cultural capital, as possessed by those with 'good' taste. Taste, however, for the members of one social group, involves a distaste for the objects which appeal to the aesthetic sense of members of another. While this is primarily exemplified by the relation between the tastes of members of different classes, Bourdieu also sees it as manifest in struggles within a group to establish a certain standard of taste in contrast to others. Were we to see cultural identity as given by a habitus characterised in terms of what members of a group share, despite class or other differences, and, in particular, in terms of features of the habitus that make its performances seem aesthetically right, others wrong, then we would seem to be left with a picture of an identity deeply embedded in its subjects by their acculturation – too deeply, perhaps, for them to articulate its standards, reflect upon them, and expose them to critique and possible rejection. The proviso, of course, is an important one: class and other differences may mean that there is *no* shared habitus of the required sort to constitute cultural identity. Here Bourdieu's notion of a field of antagonistic positions may be put into play, so that what is to count as the shared habitus of a cultural group may itself be the site of struggle. Viewed from without, then, the disquietingly functionalist sounding picture of the formation of a shared habitus is displaced by a different prospect of a variety of intersecting affinities and differences of habitus, some of which are seized upon to construct a group and its identity in one way, others for doing so in another. Here, although individuals are formed in ways that may leave them little room for change, what counts as their collective cultural identity is in no way fully determined by their upbringing, but is the result of the aesthetic reactions they, and others, have to a variety of divergent cultural trends.

Yet one might still have anxieties about such an account, adapted from Bourdieu's materials. Does it still leave too little scope for the individual to choose her own position, to accept an identity or reject it? And if it does, is this because, whatever conflict and change there may be in her culture, it is in the end facts about her acculturation which determine her position? For if it is so, then we seem drawn back into the very picture of deep cultural identity from which we have sought an escape. It is true that Bourdieu sees the habitus as giving the subject a particular sort of perspective on the world, but it would be wrong to think of this as doing more than revealing what the world would have to be like for her responses to be appropriate and to seem to her to be so. It does not explain why she responds as she does, as if her habitus were some internal causal factor. Rather, her seeing the world as she does consists in just the sort of responses that she affectedly produces. If this is so, then there is nothing of an inner cultural nature to explain her making one sort of response rather than another. There are only different patterns of regularity here. And Bourdieu thinks of them, somewhat reductively, as to be accounted for only by showing how they reflect conflictual social structures. For aesthetic contests about how to react and behave are 'political conflicts . . . for the power to impose the dominant definition of reality',[39] and in these the individual seems to have only 'a forced choice, produced by conditions of existence'.[40]

An account of identity, in this case in respect of gender and sexuality but which is closely related to Bourdieu's, is provided by Judith Butler, and it attempts to avoid the difficulty which we have just encountered and which she herself identifies in his work. Like Bourdieu, Butler sees identity as primarily a feature of the body. But, for her, identity is something *performed* through certain repetitive bodily acts, linguistic as well as non-linguistic. Certain sorts of performance, which are recognised precisely because of their repetitive character just as linguistic acts are recognised as having the meanings they do, effect the production of a particular kind of subject. To say this, however, is to say no more than that this is the kind of subject recognised as such through these standard performances. We are, for the most part, schooled into the performances through which we are identified, and they are then those that a dominant group can demand. But Butler's account has more resources than Bourdieu's for allowing exceptions to this situation.

The key to this is Butler's denial that what makes a performance successful is the authority of the performer, as it is for Bourdieu. Generalising from the case of performative speech acts, like 'I find you guilty', which achieves its result only if spoken by a judge, Bourdieu regards the social position of the agent as crucial to their action having the significance it does, and this limits the scope for meaningful change. Butler, by contrast, sees the success of a performance as residing principally in the fact of its repetitiveness. Yet its repetition in different contexts can produce different results. We might think here of the way in which a symbol of British identity, parading with Union Jacks, as in a British Legion march past on Remembrance Sunday, takes on a different significance if the bearers are skinhead supporters of the British National Party or Ulster Loyalists in Orange Order regalia. In the latter cases other markers special to their contexts combine with the flag carrying to create performances which change the identity that is being symbolised. And here this is possible only because of the significance that the flag carrying normally has, and yet here the usual authorities associated with the performance are absent.

These are not, of course, the kinds of cases that Butler is interested in, with her progressive agenda for subverting fixed gender and sexual orientation identities. But they illustrate for our purposes three important points. First, they indicate that the performances constitutive of identity are not fixed and inescapable, as features of a habitus may appear to be. They can be modified, albeit on the basis of the existing scripts that make performances meaningful. Second, they show the malleability and contingency of identities: performed in particular social and political contexts they can change both their extension – who is included – and their intension – what it is in virtue of which they are included. Third, they demonstrate how literally superficial identities can be: the different modulations of the Union Jack waving performance are small and very specific stretches of behaviour and yet they are enough to establish the identities of participants in what are, for them, at least, crucially important ways.

It may seem, however, that this is quite inadequate to account for cultural identities; surely, it may seem, there are differences of perspective on the world here that are not accommodated in this performative story. Butler is, indeed, hostile to those theories of subjectivity which postulate such perspectives. Yet even if this rejection is regarded as too general, she may still be right that the performances constitutive of collective identities do not correlate with any shared perspectives. True, in our examples, there are different beliefs held by the different identity-group performers, but nothing as wide ranging as different perspectives seem to be involved. How, then, might the attractions of one kind of identity formation rather than another be explained, if not by the way one perspective on the world presents a different range of things as desirable than does another?

Butler's answer to the question 'to what extent does knowing a subject require/presuppose a passionate attachment to subjection?'[41] is, in part, a psycho-analytic one, but it is grounded in the idea that desires themselves are constituted by performances in which our bodies are differentially bound to stimuli. Marching in one way rather than another is a response to different objects and expresses different pleasures – of gravity, of defiance or of triumph, for example. Yet all we have here, it might be claimed in Aristotelian vein, are different kinds of unimpeded activity. To be able, if only in imagination, to act like this *is* to see the world in a certain way. There is no legitimate conception of so seeing it which *explains* the actions.

The accounts of cultural identity which we have just been considering deny, in different ways, that it is a deep-going feature of the self. Reflection upon the manner of its formation should lead us to see its contingency and, in particular, its dependence upon processes which do not necessarily tend towards serving our interests. We are then able to look at ourselves from without, as it were, and all we see are certain patterns of regular behaviour shared, to a greater or lesser extent, with others whose culture consists in doing things this way rather than in a different one. So viewed, a cultural identity provides thus far no reason for political mobilisation.

Notes

1. Robert Young, *Torn Halves* (Manchester: Manchester University Press, 1996), p. 116.
2. Julia Kristeva, *Strangers to Ourselves* (New York, NY: Columbia University Press, 1991), p. 192.

3. Gustave Le Bon, quoted in Paul Lawrence, *Nationalism* (Harlow: Pearson Longman, 2005), pp. 74–5.
4. Wilfred Trotter, *Instincts of the Herd in Peace and War* (London: Benn, 1947), p. 150.
5. Ibid. p. 179.
6. Quoted in Peter Gay, *Freud* (London: Macmillan, 1989), p. 405.
7. Sigmund Freud, *Complete Psychological Works* (London: Hogarth Press, 1953–74), vol. XVIII, p. 116.
8. Ibid. p. 103.
9. Ibid. p. 102.
10. Sigmund Freud, *Works*, vol. XXI, p. 13.
11. David Miller, 'In defence of nationality', in P. Gilbert and P. Gregory (eds), *Nations, Cultures and Markets* (Aldershot: Avebury, 1994).
12. John McGarry and Brendan O'Leary, *Explaining Northern Ireland* (Oxford: Blackwell, 1995), p. 253.
13. John Cash, *Identity, Ideology and Conflict* (Cambridge: Cambridge University Press, 1996), p. 6.
14. Ibid. p. 76.
15. Ibid. p. 111.
16. Ibid. p. 154.
17. Jürgen Habermas, *Knowledge and Human Interests* (Boston, MA: Beacon, 1971), p. 233.
18. Jacques Lacan, *The Four Fundamental Concepts of Psycho-Analysis* (Harmondsworth: Penguin, 1979), p. 203.
19. Julia Kristeva, *Powers of Horror* (New York, NY: Columbia University Press, 1982).
20. Freud, *Works*, vol. XVII, pp. 217–56.
21. Ibid. p. 236.
22. Ibid. p. 245.
23. Freud, *Works*, vol. XXII, p. 57.
24. Kristeva, *Strangers to Ourselves*, p. 192.
25. Ibid. p. 192.
26. Ibid. p. 191.
27. Ibid. p. 1.
28. Julia Kristeva, *Nations Without Nationalism* (New York, NY: Columbia University Press, 1993), p. 50.
29. Ibid. p. 52.
30. Ibid. p. 8.
31. 'Manifesto of the Communist Party', in L. S. Feuer (ed.), *Marx and Engels: Basic Writings on Politics and Philosophy* (New York, NY: Doubleday, 1959).
32. Ernest Gellner, *Nations and Nationalism* (Oxford: Blackwell, 1983), p. 6.

33. Benedict Anderson, *Imagined Communities* (London: Verso, 1991), p. 6.
34. Ibid. p. 12.
35. Louis Althusser, *Lenin and Philosophy* (New York, NY: Monthly Review Press, 1971), p. 154.
36. Ibid. p. 162.
37. Pierre Bourdieu, *The Logic of Practice* (Cambridge: Polity, 1990), p. 87.
38. Ibid. p. 78.
39. Pierre Bourdieu, 'The production of belief', in R. Collins (ed.), *Media, Culture and Society* (Beverley Hills, CA: Sage, 1986), pp. 154–5.
40. Pierre Bourdieu, *Distinction* (Cambridge, MA: Harvard University Press, 1984), p. 178.
41. Judith Butler, 'Subjection, resistance, resignification', in J. Rajchman (ed.), *The Identity in Question* (New York, NY: Routledge, 1995), p. 244.

7
The Art of Identity

The Recognition of Identity

Insistence that collective cultural identity is not a deep identity may seem untrue to the phenomenology of identity – to the way people feel about their cultural identifications, in particular to their attachments to them and the way features of their culture evoke such attachments. Now it is widely accepted that cultural identities, and in particular national identities, are constituted, at least in part, by distinctive artistic productions – literature, painting, music and so on – to which the members of a cultural group will have responses of a sort not shared by those outside it. I shall ask, then, what the nature of these responses is and how they might lead people to think of the relevant art works as, in some sense, their own. And what I suggest is that these aesthetic responses are a model for those reactions to surface features of a culture that lead to identification and attachment.

I shall start with a well-known incident that took place during the formation of a modern Irish identity – the adverse reaction to J. M. Synge's play *The Playboy of the Western World*, when it was performed in Dublin in 1907. The play sparked a riot when the word 'shift' (for a female undergarment) was used, thus supposedly outraging the sensibilities of its Irish Catholic audience. There was, of course, a wider background. Synge was a Protestant Anglo-Irishman, a member of the class held to be responsible for Ireland's subjection to England and for the impoverishment of its inhabitants. The cultural thrust of Irish nationalism had been the 'de-Anglicisation' of Ireland through the replacement of English by Irish as the nation's language. Furthermore, although officially religion may have been decoupled from national identity, the Catholicism of the majority of its inhabitants led nationalists to insist that 'the Irish nation is *de facto* a Catholic nation',[1] a fact to which its Protestant members were expected to defer. One writer made the connection thus: 'English is the language of infidelity . . . The sooner we discard English and revive our own language, the better off the faith will be in Ireland.'[2] Such nationalists resented the way that Anglo-Irish authors like Synge and Yeats depicted an English-speaking identity; for what Synge's plays attempted to do was to capture the Hiberno-English speech patterns he had heard while staying on the Aran Islands and elsewhere in the west of Ireland. What the rioters were really objecting to, then, was this alternative conception of Irish identity.

The irony of the situation is, as I have mentioned, that it was precisely this alternative conception which prevailed, and which prevailed in part because of the response that later Irish audiences made to Synge's plays and to the other literary productions of Anglo-Irish authors. It was, one might say, a response of identification with the characters presented in these works. But in what did this identification consist? Micheál MacLiammóir suggests that what really shook the audience of *The Playboy* was 'the unaccustomed spectacle of truth',[3] so that what eventually happened, on this account, would be that Irish people saw themselves as accurately represented in this depiction. Generalising then, *this* answer to our question, as to what sort of response members of a cultural group have to works involved in constituting their identity, would be that it is one of recognition of a pre-existent identity, of which the works provide them with a keener reflective sense.

The obvious focus for such a supposed recognition is the language of the characters in Synge's play. It is not enough here for Synge to have had an accurate ear for some version of Hiberno-English, but the language must also be a medium in which his audience could, so to speak, feel comfortable. To be recognisable it had to be sympathetic. For earlier Anglo-Irish authors, like Somerville and Ross, with an equally accurate ear, had satirised the native Irish through contrasting their diction with the serious speech of English characters. Synge's language, by contrast, realises Oscar Wilde's observation that the Irish took from the English 'their language and added new beauties to it'.[4] Synge's characters give celebrated speeches like:

> It's little you'll think my love's a poacher's, or an earl's itself, when you'll feel my two hands stretched around you, and squeezing kisses on your puckered lips, till I'd feel a kind of pity for the Lord God is all ages sitting lonesome in His golden chair.[5]

This is a language whose beauty – and irony – make it a fitting medium for relationships of a sensual intensity that shocked early audiences, yet it came to enchant later ones. But was their reaction really simply recognition of the way they actually spoke, at least at their best as it were?

It would be risky, to start with, to assume that Synge does accurately reproduce the speech patters of western Ireland. It was criticised as 'contrived literary stuff, entirely unrepresentative of peasant speech'.[6] And, even if representative of that, it certainly could not capture the very various forms of the spoken language across Ireland. Instead it came to represent a stereotype of Irish speech which allowed critics like Flann O'Brien to remark that:

> nothing in the whole galaxy of fake is comparable with Synge . . . and now the curse has come upon us because I have personally met in the streets of Ireland persons who are clearly out of Synge's plays. They talk and dress like that and damn the drink they'll swally but the mug of porter in the long nights.[7]

Irish speakers were, in other words, shaping their own diction to that of the characters in Synge's plays. Identification was not simply recognition, but adoption.

Yet if this is so, it might be objected, responses to Synge's play by Irish audiences are recognition of a pre-existing fact *now*, even if they were not *then*. A distinction must be drawn, and this we must grant, between the formation of a national identity and its maintenance. Whatever is the case in the former, it may be suggested, in the latter members of the nation need to be able to recognise themselves in certain focal art works, for example in those that present them with what is their national way of speaking. There are several ways to reply to this. One is to observe that Flann O'Brien's 'persons who are clearly out of Synge's plays' are still an exception in a continuing variety of speech modes. And Synge's language probably now sounds rather quaint as these modes inevitably change.

But what I want to challenge is the assumption behind the simple recognitional account that something could be identified as a distinctively Irish way of speaking and then matched up with Synge's language. For this presupposes that we do already have a criterion of similarity across the different forms of Irish speech that make them Irish in the required sense. And this is a sense in which they are all heard as other than alien by the Irish. Now no doubt it is a very complex process through which this sort of similarity is constituted, but it depends upon different cases being classed as the same, and that in turn depends upon the existence of some technique for making such a classification of similarity and difference. One technique is to employ 'objects of comparison', or samples with which cases are compared, and arguably the sorts of stereotype Synge and others produced function in this way. They function, that is to say, as scarlet functions as a paradigm of red, so that were we not to have such colour paradigms but other ones, then the way we classified colours as similar and different would be otherwise than it actually is.

I am not here making the *grossly* implausible claim that Irish voices would not have been heard as alike without Synge. There is a long tradition of representations of Irish talk, mainly by English authors, if these were indeed needed to mark out something distinctive. But this sort of classification is typically an outsider's one. What we are concerned with here, though, is an insider's classification which they might express as 'the way we talk', which is why it must be sympathetic. And finding something that can be pointed to as a sample of this establishes a sense to 'we', namely as fellow speakers in the same way of talking. Then an individual's identification involved in responding to such a model as provided by an art work is, as we shall see later, one which presupposes this collective identification. But here I observe only that for the sample to fulfil its function it must, of course, be usable by the people for whom it is intended generally. There must be, that is to say, some general 'agreement in judgement' as to the relevant similarities and differences. An art work that fails to provide such a usable paradigm cannot, at least in just this way, provide a focus for cultural identity.

What authors like Synge provided, I am claiming, were samples of Irishness, which, together with many others, established the required kind of criteria of similarity. The catch is, however, that something is accepted as such a criterion not only to facilitate classification, but for quite other purposes. That these samples were initially rejected indicates how crucial these purposes are. For though they were then regarded as travesties of how the Irish actually spoke, they were principally rejected as models of how the Irish *should* speak and relate to each other. This is not just because they supposedly should speak Irish, not English, and observe strict Catholic moral codes, but because they should not be as unrestrained and colourful, so to speak, as Synge's exuberantly fluent peasants. What is objected to is the sort of appeal that this might have.

So what I am suggesting, then, is that, in addition to providing samples that establish criteria of similarity, Synge and others offered models of how to be Irish. And this, I believe, is a very general phenomenon. National literatures and others associated with particular cultural groups set up models of how to behave as well as depictions of behaviour, usually flagged up as good or bad. Painting provides models not only of how to look, but of how and what to see, and so on. This is principally why the simple account of recognition I have described cannot work. For what is needed if a model is being offered is acceptance of the model, which is distinct from recognition of a representation. In the case of Synge's play, what is needed is a continuing acceptance of its characters' way of speaking as a medium for talk and for relationships, and this, of course, cannot just be a matter of recognising some facts. It requires not so much an acknowledgement that things are so as an approval of their being so, a people's approval of their being so for them as Irish. An identificatory response requires such an acceptance, which is why, as I mentioned near the outset, the representation must be sympathetic. That is to say, it must offer a model capable of acceptance.

Despite my dismissal of what I am calling the simple recognitional account of identification, someone might justifiably object that the Irish might have thought that they were indeed recognising themselves in *The Playboy*. But how can this be, if, as I am arguing, the cultural identity in question is constituted by just such identificatory responses, rather than being something pre-given, with which a comparison can be made that leads to recognition and identification? Why did the Irish, in fact, respond in just this way even as they were at the same time realising that they were hearing something quite striking and, in a sense, unfamiliar? So it is not as if they were hearing a recording of their speech which they could match up with the way they spoke and straight-forwardly acknowledge its accuracy. For Synge's way of presenting their speech is striking precisely because it is *not* something they had previously heeded among themselves. It is, so to say, more brightly coloured, as scarlet is than the colours of ordinary life. How, then, can it be thought of as recognition, when this cannot be construed on what I term the simple recognitional account?

This case is parallel, I suggest, to very many psycho-logical states, like wanting, intending, expecting, meaning something, believing, and so on. In all these it is often true that whether I am in the psychological state depends solely on whether I make the right response to some situation, so that nothing prior to and independent of its occurrence constitutes the fact of my being in that state. Yet I take my response as indicating that I was in the state all along; that, for a fairly vivid type of example, I wanted this colour shirt all along when I see it in the shop, even though I had had no prior image of it. It is usual in these cases to attribute a disposition to make the relevant response in the appro-priate circumstances; usual, but entirely unhelpful, since it does nothing to explain the response in the sort of case we are considering. Analogously, the attribution of a prior identity similarly conceived fails to explain the cultural response. We make the attribution simply on the basis of the later response. And it is the fact that we attribute the identity as a pre-existing one which licenses us to think of these responses as recognitional, in just the same way as responding to the shirt I see as just the colour I wanted counts as recognising what I wanted. By contrast, a change in my tastes may lead me to want a colour of shirt I would never previously have countenanced, and a similar collective change can lead to a modification in a people's cultural identity.

What I am arguing here, then, is that we cannot easily distinguish identity from a sense of identity, as if we already have an identity determined by certain facts about us, and then came to have a sense of that identity through reflection upon these facts. This is the picture we get from the simple recognitional account. Instead, identity is dependent upon a sense of identity on our present account even though it is attributed as pre-existing it, in this case, because identity derives from the identificatory responses we make and which express that sense of identity.

But the idea of a sense of identity slips uneasily between perception and sentiment. On the former understanding people supposedly grasp their affinity, as the Irish hear in Synge's play the distinctive and shared way in which they speak. On the latter, they resolve to relate to each other as a single and separate people, as the Irish see the language and relationships in *The Playboy* as a model for theirs. And the question of what sort of voice national mores are to be conducted in is, of course, a question calling for decisions, continuing decisions, rather than just a question of fact.

This uneasy slippage between a sense of collective identity as perception and as sentiment or attitude arises from the character of the response to cultural foci itself. This counts as a perception of who one already is because of the kind of identification one makes with what the works present. But this identification involves an attitude one might have withheld, because the identity in question might not have been what one wanted to have; and to the extent that one resists it, it is an identity one does not have. But to revise it involves not making the responses that go with the identity, rather than finding oneself making them and blaming oneself for it. A willing identification is an attitude to what the work presents in which one finds what one wants to be in it, though that this is what one wanted to be may not be something one previously knew. Sentiment and perception, then, are intimately connected because to recognise who one is, in the sort of case under discussion, is to embrace it.

What does seem to be the case is that the element of decision involved in identification is occluded, so that all that *seems* to be involved to those making the identifying response is recognition of what is already so. What, we may ask, explains this? I do not here wish to pursue the Freudian theory of identification as a form of wish fulfilment, in which the subject's projection of himself on to a character appears to him as involuntary and, as such, is a source of pleasure which, were he to acknowledge his own part in it, would not be forthcoming. Rather, I do wish to pick up the idea of pleasure involved in identification in the form of the *appreciation* of the art work to which an identificatory response is made. The question I turn to, then, is what is it to have just *this* sort of appreciative reaction; what is it for a work to have this sort of appeal, as against the kind of appeal it might have as an art work for just anyone?

The Ancient Music of Ireland

So far I may seem to have been generalising wildly from my Synge's *The Playboy* example, where talk of identification gets a natural foothold from the kind of response the play invites in presenting the language the characters use as a model of the national idiom, and through it of the relationships of members of the nation. But though we cannot talk in quite this way of identification where many other art works are involved – with music or painting for example – there is, I shall want to claim, a process that is analogous to this, operating in cultural group members' responses even to these. Again I shall stick with the Irish, and again in the sense that this word imputes a cultural identity. The question I want to address is the nature of the appeal that various canonical art works have in virtue of which we can speak of their audience identifying with them and in so doing entertaining a sense of identity.

The problem here is to distinguish this sort of appeal from the appeal that the same art work might well have to someone who does not share the specified cultural identity. What is the difference, we must ask, between mere appreciation and appreciation which involves the kind of identification involved when someone responds to it qua member of a cultural group?

I have been gesturing at this answer, namely that the work must present something as, in a specific sense to be unpacked, their own. Another author in the Irish literary renaissance, George Moore, put the matter thus: some of one's own country's art may be 'no more than a daisy in the great flower garden of the world's art; but a daisy that is your own is perhaps better than a sunflower that is somebody else's'.[8] Something widely popular outside Ireland, but which has this sort of significance within, is Irish music. How might the Irish hear it differently from others?

A well known Irish air is 'Danny Boy' which first appeared in George Petrie's *Ancient Music of Ireland* in 1855, taken down in Limavady near Derry from an itinerant piper. Airs like this have characteristically plaintive melodies with their unexpected high notes rising from an undertow of low ones. We know what sort of feeling concepts to bring to bear to hear them appropriately, and not, say, as cloyingly sentimental. But in the Irish context they have a special significance of the fear of loss, and of hope against that fear. To hear them as Irish airs, as not only the Irish can do, is to bring such ideas to them. Similar observations could be made about Irish jigs. Their lazy rolling rhythm, despite their speed, brings to mind the kind of dance for which they are often played, and the idea of this needs to be brought to bear upon them to hear them as the Irish would. And to bring it to bear is very naturally to have thoughts of the same sort of exuberance as is expressed by Synge's peasants and to enter into their sorts of feelings, as with the airs we entertain contrasting feelings. All this produces in us, I suggest, what Barrie Falk calls 'a reflective state of the will'.[9]

Falk's example is the state caused by seeing an avalanche – the kind of thing Kant classifies as sublime. It is, he says,

> a speculative or imaginative state, in which one reflects on the various modes of behaviour open to one, the various kinds of situation one is likely to encounter; and, in the course of that imaginary, one finds in oneself a susceptibility to certain kinds of reason for action, rather than others.

In this state, he goes on,

> the susceptibility to certain kinds of reason for action which the avalanche has induced in me will rob . . . other concerns of their power to draw my attention . . . [for] my attention does not merely return to the avalanche but is *drawn* back to it as the focus of my currently imaginatively overriding concerns.[10]

I want to apply this to the experience of certain sorts of music. With the jig, say, we are moved in imagination to make merry; with the airs, by contrast, to concern ourselves with the problems from which the jigs are an escape. And it is no accident that a typical Irish music session is a mixture of dance music and airs. What we have here then, is a characteristically Irish movement of feeling which leads the Irish to think of the music as their own.

The structure of identification with works like Irish airs and jigs seems, then, to be like this. People bring various thoughts to bear on the music which enable them to hear it in a certain way. The music is hospitable to common features of these thoughts, and people with common experiences, like the Irish, will be able to bring to bear sufficiently similar thoughts to hear it in the same way – though others, through imagination, can, to some extent, do so too. The process I describe enables the Irish airs to capture common feelings, yet feelings linked in the way suggested to limited rather than, in some sense, universal experiences. That is why they are folk music, the music of a particular people with which they identify. What is involved here is, I want to say, a *feeling* of identification, not just an acknowledgement that members of the group make simply because they *know* that some art work does have special cultural significance for them. That could involve no feelings at all or, if it does, feelings of attachment or the like that are extraneous to their appreciation of the art work and not an aspect of it. Let us recall, then, that we are taking the feelings involved in appreciation to involve reflective states of the will, in the sense of imagined reorderings of motivational priorities.

In such reflective states, we may recall, we are *drawn* back to their objects, as the foci of what currently takes priority as an imagined concern. So in listening to their music, I suggest, the Irish are drawn to it as focusing just such concerns of theirs, and this is an emotional experience. Their identification with the music is something that is *felt*, then, because they are drawn to it in this way. And this gives an answer, I suggest, to our earlier question of why our own part in selecting models of identity is occluded in favour of a supposed recognition of who we are. It is because we are drawn to the model we select, and this is something we feel, that the fact of acceptance and the possibility of resistance are obscured. The concerns which currently take priority imaginatively drive out the others that one might have entertained. And this prevents the opportunity for choice from being grasped, and with it the chosen character of this model of feeling rather than some other.

Yet this does not fully explain why it is just these models to which a people are drawn; why, for example, it is with jigs, airs and so forth that the Irish experience the sort of identification they do, while analogous forms of folk music do not play this sort of role for others, for the English, say; and why others besides the Irish could bring the appropriate thoughts to bear, but not identify with the music. No doubt there are historical or sociological explanations, but these are not what we seek here. What we are looking for instead is an account of what it is for certain art works to have the kind of appeal they do to one cultural group rather than another. So let us return to the idea that they induce in people specific reflective states of the will.

Now reflective states of the will like this can have different uses, or applications, for they can be more or less connected with actual rather than merely imagined willings. The sort of feelings associated with a sad tune, for example, lead us to think of many things as unimportant compared with the possibilities of suffering a loss. But its consequent significance for someone depends upon their own vulnerability to such suffering. Then it has, we may say, a more serious use for them than it does for others. They can identify with it as expressing their own feelings, as someone else, whose life does not provide much occasion for them, cannot. And the same goes, I suggest, for the music and other artistic productions that are special to a particular people. They can identify with it because they actually undergo the feelings it expresses, and this can be the case even though the availability of those feelings as shared in this form is mediated by just these productions. So again, I want to see these feelings as shaped by the art works viewed as expressing them, rather than pre-existing them. What is pre-existent are the circumstances that make the serious application of reflective states possible.

The members of a cultural group experience their art works as their own, then, because they have a serious use for them, a use which engages shared feelings – feelings which are only coincidentally shared by others outside the group, not shared in virtue of who they are. But it is because members take the works to be specifically theirs through expressing these feelings that they expect fellow members to share their appreciation and thereby to make the same identificatory responses. It is to this aspect that we now turn.

A Historical People?

The sort of identity of which identification with cultural works offers some sense is, of course, a cultural identity, so that, as I have assumed, it is 'the way *we* are', not just 'the way *I* am', that the work so responded to seems to reflect. But how is it that the identification can have this collective character? It comes to something more, I maintain, than each individual's confidence that other members of the group are likely to make similar responses, though this is a part of it. Music, drama and so forth are shared experiences, so that, for example, in an Irish session, the audience's mood changes as a piper moves from a medley of jigs to a slow air. But the reason for an individual's confidence that his response is shared is surely not his noticing such facts about collective behaviour. It is, rather, that he takes himself to be making, in some sense, the *right* response to the music, the right response, that is to say, for him as a member of the group. Yet for him to respond qua member he must be able, in general, to make what is deemed the right response. And for this there must be standards of correctness, I suggest, not just statistical norms, to which he will, in general, be conforming his responses.

What, though, can count as a right response, and how could this be relative to a particular group – and a group constituted, in part, by its members responding to art works in accordance with these standards? In 'The communicability of feeling',[11] Barrie Falk discusses Kant's conception of 'exemplary' feelings like those I have before a beautiful object. Here the feeling is not, like pain say, simply dependent upon properties of myself, for the feeling is one that anyone else will have, leaving aside individual deviations. Thus, for Kant, judgements of taste claim *universal* assent, not because they bring their objects under concepts, but because they rely on the fact of shared responses. And because of this agreement in judgement the responses can be viewed as responses to the way things are in the world, just as if shared concepts were being applied. Falk generalises Kant's conclusion to a range of other feelings, for example of pity for an old man, which constitutes an awareness of what is the case because they are the feelings anyone might be expected to have in these circumstances. But to say they are the right feelings, and hence communicable to others like myself, is to say that the world really is as the feelings reveal it to be. In the case of pity for the old man, what is revealed is the bleakness of the world which induces, as Falk puts it, a 'stilling of the will'. And Falk goes on to claim that 'the creation of art is in part a response to the poignancy which truths of this sort possess'.[12] It is the emotions we feel in response to such art works with which we are concerned here.

The rightness of these responses for members of a cultural group cannot be given quite the same sort of treatment that Falk suggests; for the standards concerning them are specifically for members of the group rather than for people generally. What sense can we make of this? We can be helped here, I suggest, by noting Falk's observation that pity might not be the only appropriate response to the old man. Another possibility is, he writes, 'a kind of tense indifference', in which I steel my will rather than becoming dispirited. For, as he puts it, 'being in the world is like many things and it is like them simultaneously'.[13] Here, then, is one possible idea, namely that, though there are many ways to view the world, and different art works present a diversity of them, some of these ways are in some sense right for some people and the corresponding art works are readily appreciated by them. Then the cultural standards on which we are trying to get a handle are those that pick out which ways are right for members of the culture and which regulate their responses accordingly. But what can it be for some privileged set of views of the world, presented by culturally specific art works, to be right for that culture's members? Here we can draw upon Heidegger's notion that 'to be a work' – a work of art, that is – 'means to set up a world';[14] and Heidegger gives as an example a Greek temple in its landscape which 'fits together and at the same time gathers around itself the unity of those paths and relations' which belong to a 'historical people',[15] and which thereby sets up their world. Heidegger's assumption here is that a people's world is not something given by facts about them, as if an art work might somehow accord with these facts. It is, rather, the way things are for them in virtue of their material and social practices, their 'paths and relations'. On this sort of account, then, the rightness of certain art works for them – like the temple for the Greeks – could not consist in its relation to facts, but rather in the use it has in showing how things are for them. And this it does by bringing unity and cohesion to this otherwise incoherent multiplicity – a unity only possible in its being a work to which those for whom things are so can respond in the same way. And this is a unity that the people's life would not have had without the work that evokes this shared response.

The temple belonged to the Greeks as especially theirs because it was their paths and relations to which it brought unity. And the unity it brings, I think Heidegger would want to say, is not that of some specific conceptualisation. It is the sort of unity that the work of art brings to life as a whole, to what being in the world is like, as Falk puts it, not to what particular projects or relationships are like. To grasp how this is *is* to respond in a certain way, as grasping the beauty of a picture is. It is to have the appropriate feelings; and the appropriate feelings for people with one sort of life will be different from those for others, for it is their life that the work unifies in this way. Even if we think of a people, in this sense, as constituted as such by their art works, there must still be something else they share – a life. But the relation between the works and the life is not one of correspondence; so that it is no accident that Heidegger chooses a non-representational art form – architecture – to make his point. It is, one might even say, coherence. For the temple is part of life, as all our commerce with art works is, and it is at the same time what unifies that life, in the sense of giving 'men their outlook on themselves',[16] through the place it has in their lives.

If we turn back to Falk's notion of responsive feelings as reflective states of the will, and my own application of this to the responses of a particular cultural group's members as more serious, as I put it, than those of others, then we can see how this relates to the foregoing suggestions. For the life of a people, their 'paths and relations', has a characteristic shape in virtue of the way certain motivations take priority over others in various circumstances. This is exemplified in the way they face up to their cares or play them down, seize on opportunities for pleasure or pass them by, and so on. Their music, say, can give a shape and a direction to these movements. So can their literature in its forms and figures, its possibilities of tone and colour, which are continuous with the way these movements of the will are expressed in ordinary speech. It is in this sense that I want to say that Synge's *The Playboy* provides some shape for social relations among the Irish. Its acceptance as that is a matching up of its audience's motivational priorities to the reflective states of the will that the language of its characters induces. Its rightness for them consists not in its *reflecting* antecedent priorities, but in the possibility of those states being serious for them. And they can be serious only within the patterns of social relationship they characterise – intense, dedicated, jokey, or whatever. And these are among the 'paths and relations' which the art work unifies for them.

All this takes us, of course, a long way from the universalist aesthetic theory of Kant, and some may think too far for the responses to art invoked to be genuinely *aesthetic* at all, rather than depending upon interests that make the judgements merely subjective. What I have attempted to suggest is that this degree of commonality does entitle us to speak of a shared aesthetic, and that the fact that the scope of those who share these judgements is limited, in the way it is, is necessary for the judgements to do the work of constituting something common to those who make them, which provides an identity not shared by others.[17] The limited universality of a cultural group's aesthetic judgements, their acknowledgement that their appreciation may not be shared by outsiders but can be expected among themselves, this is what is necessary for that appreciation to involve identification. For the fact that, along with these others, I appreciate this work is taken to tell me what I am like, what I share with them. This is what constitutes, I suggest, the sense of identity to which such an appreciative response gives rise. And the kind of appreciation involved is important for this. For it is, I suggest, that this consists in a serious reflective state of the will that tells me, not just that I am the kind of person who likes these sorts of art works, but that they have the sort of significance for my life that I have gestured at. This is a more important fact about me, and arguably a defining one. But all this, I have tried to argue, can be handled without resorting to the sorts of essential difference between members of different cultural groups that a Herderian relativising of Kant's theory might suggest.

Having erected this rather Byzantine structure, I want to end by destabilising it. Or rather, perhaps, to suggest that if the foregoing conclusions are correct then some of the unquestioned assumptions on which we have been proceeding need to be rejected. For I have happily spoken of cultural groups, membership of which confers identity, and, following most authors, have taken national identity as an example of this. But the slipperiness of my references to the 'Irish' here may already have aroused suspicion. Sometimes I have seemed to include the Irish outside of Ireland – Irish-American lovers of Irish music, say – while at others my references to Irish speech as a marker of identity have implicitly excluded them. The fact is that the idea of more or less homogeneous and discrete cultural groups has, at best, very limited application, and certainly Irishness cannot pick out such a group. There are just too many competing criteria for this to be the case.

The reason for this is, I believe, something that can be seen from the consequences of my account together with some banal sociological observations. I claimed that the responses to its foci required of putative members of a cultural group have to be what I termed serious if they are to be different from the responses just anyone might make. And they can be serious only within the social relationships to which the cultural works bring the sort of unity that is involved in their setting up a world. But the picture that this Heideggerian account seems to presuppose is of fairly clearly delimited networks of social relationship, in particular those that involve following the 'paths' of a 'historical people'. Yet, sociologically, things just are not like this. The different extensions that can be attributed to the term 'Irish' illustrate the point. There is no single Irish identity, just a variety of fairly indeterminate identities depending upon which collections of people are being regarded as Irish. The sorts of relationship that there are between members of them will vary and perhaps at best, in the most restricted case, will talk of 'paths' be apposite. In this situation, how serious members' responses to cultural foci will be also differ, so that how dissimilar their self-identifications are to mere appreciation will vary too.

The moral to draw from this is that insofar as shared aesthetic appreciation might really sort people out into different cultural groups it can do so only on the basis of relationships they have with each other, and whether they have such relationships will depend upon the circumstances by which they are thrown together and how they react to them. To appreciate the commonality of their shared circumstances may require a shared aesthetic, but it requires more than this. The sort of collective self-identification that people might make simply on the basis of sharing an aesthetic does not so far require more. It may be, to repeat the phrase, mere lip service even when aesthetic feeling accompanies it and, while for political purposes this may be sufficient, it is insufficient to give such a cultural identity the importance for members which is often claimed for it in support of such purposes. For self-identifications may, in passing enthusiasms, reflect no serious common feelings, which only a common life in shared circumstances can evoke. And a shared aesthetic can be delusory, leading people to think of their common feelings as having a significance in bringing them together that their real relationships belie, much as 'our tune' can mislead a romantic but ill-suited couple. Such delusions, stemming from shared reactions to art works or other objects of aesthetic appreciation, can be fostered in pursuit of political purposes. This is, I suggest, the very stuff of cultural identity politics.

Notes

1. *The Leader*, 27 July 1901, quoted in Conor Cruise O'Brien, *Ancestral Voices* (Dublin: Poolbeg, 1994), p. 59.
2. Father Cathaoir O'Braonain, quoted in Tim Pat Coogan, *Ireland in the Twentieth Century* (London: Hutchinson, 2003), p. 705.
3. Micheál MacLiammóir, 'Introduction', in J. M. Synge, *Plays, Poems and Prose* (London: Dent, 1958), p. viii.
4. Quoted in H. M. Hyde, *Oscar Wilde* (London: Methuen, 1976), p. 69.
5. J. M. Synge, 'Playboy of the Western World', in J. M. Synge, *Plays, Poems and Prose* (London: Dent, 1958), Act 3, p. 155.
6. John Ervine, quoted in D. Kiberd, *Synge and the Irish Language* (London: Macmillan, 1993), p. 174.
7. Flann O'Brien, quoted in A. Warner, *A Guide to Anglo-Irish Literature* (Dublin: Gill and Macmillan, 1981), p. 161.
8. George Moore, *Hail and Farewell: Ave* (London: Heinemann, 1937), p. vi.
9. Barrie Falk, 'Having what we want', *Proceedings of the Aristotelian Society*, vol. 91 (1990–1), p. 175.
10. Ibid. pp. 175–6.
11. Barrie Falk, 'The communicability of feeling', in E. Schaper (ed.), *Pleasure, Preference and Value* (Cambridge: Cambridge University Press, 1983).
12. Ibid. p. 80.
13. Ibid. p. 78.
14. M. Heidegger, 'The origin of the work of art', in D. F. Krell (ed.), *Martin Heidegger: Basic Writings* (London: Routledge, 1978), p. 170.
15. Ibid. p. 168.
16. Ibid. p. 169.
17. Cp. Kennan Ferguson, *The Politics of Judgement* (Lanham: Lexington Books, 1999), ch. 2.

8
The Ethics of Identity

The Value of Identity

Apologists for a politics of identity often speak in terms of the *value* of cultural identity. If the line of argument I have been pursuing is correct then cultural identity, in the sense of membership of a cultural group, has, in itself, no value for people. If they do not qua members have a deep identity of the sort I have tried to characterise, then there is no need for a cultural identity so far as their psychological functioning is concerned, and so such an identity does not have value in supplying such a need. The Herderian notion that there is such a value is used to justify the political recognition of cultural identity and thus its protection, preservation and so on. But, as I have been arguing, such attempted justifications have foundations on sand and rest on confusions. Rather than passing them in review, then, I shall run through some of the assimilations that such justifications commonly trade on.

First, cultural components are, of course, important parts of individual identities, in the sense of what make people the sorts of individuals they are. No doubt I would be a different sort of person from the one I am if my native tongue was not English or if I had not acquired the educated

English I have, as against my local dialect. No doubt, too, this language is important for me: I should not be writing these words without it or thinking these thoughts. But none of this implies either that I have a cultural identity in terms of membership of a cultural group of the wide-ranging sort we have been considering, partly defined by language use; or that, if indeed I have – being English say – then *this* has value for me. Any useful account of what is of value for me has already been given in saying how the language is; and, incidentally, my use of the language does not require membership of the group that provides my putative identity. I can use the language without any such membership and lose nothing by it.

The same considerations seem to me to apply to values, history or whatever. An individual can derive whatever benefits they confer in making a life effective and fulfilling without the fact, if it is a fact, that they identify him culturally being involved. There is, however, an argument against this that needs disposing of. It is that we cannot in this way separate out the components of identity, since they work together to constitute a cultural system; and this, of course, is a Herderian view. We find it assumed in many recent defences of identity politics of which Will Kymlicka's is canonical,[1] and it is recognisable as what anthropologists refer to as functionalism. Functionalism holds that individuals internalise culture as a guiding force which holds members together in an integrated society. Interference with their cultural identity thus threatens that society; so its value lies in its integrative role for individuals, without which, as we noticed earlier, they would, on this account, be anomic or confused. Kymlicka and other liberal theorists give a particular twist to this argument by claiming that the value which would be threatened is autonomy – the capacity to make choices that are genuinely one's own and which hang together in a coherent life.

We can see that Kymlicka's and similar arguments

involve functionalist assumptions from the fact that the national statehood which he advocates in some circumstances to protect cultures is justified as preventing *externally* imposed change, while Kymlicka has no problem with *internally* initiated change. But this distinction presupposes the implausible view of cultures as clearly delimited closed systems which we have been at pains to oppose. Imposition, whether external or internal, is a threat to autonomy, while changes from whatever source may or may not manifest autonomous processes. If the value for individuals in a culture of the sort Kymlicka wishes to have protected is autonomy, however, then it is evident that this is a cardinal value only in certain sorts of culture anyway, and not a general one that can, without question begging, be invoked for the protection of cultural identity so construed.[2]

There is an argument to the conclusion that cultural identity is valuable for someone which does not involve functionalist assumptions but which also sees an overall culture as what makes possible the goods that cultural components deliver to individuals. Charles Taylor, for example, holds that 'a cultural good may . . . exist only to the extent that it is commonly prized',[3] and he views this as happening within a cultural framework which is thus presupposed in the existence of valuable cultural components. Taylor believes that the framework is therefore itself valuable in delivering them. But even if that framework is valued for this it does not follow that membership of the culture and the identity which it supposedly confers are valuable. There may be other components of the culture which are disvalued or the identity it offers may militate against other goods. Thus, the poet Yeats clearly valued the English culture which had produced the language in which he wrote, but, unlike many of his Anglo-Irish contemporaries, rejected membership of it in favour of an Irish identity which, he thought, acknowledged the value of relationships with those among whom he lived, some of whom spoke Irish.

Arguments like Kymlicka's or Taylor's which regard membership of a culture as valuable for individuals both tend to conflate cultures with communities in a way we have already warned against. Kymlicka's own conception of a 'societal culture'[4] which involves social and political institutions as well as a language and history is particularly vulnerable to this conflation. But the value of membership of a community for individuals is quite a different thing from that claimed for cultural identity. To start with, membership of a community is intrinsically valuable, for the sorts of relationship which it involves are valued by members and, whatever their reservations about their particular community, we cannot conceive of this being otherwise. But it need not, of course, be a cultural community which provides these relationships, nor is there anything specifically valuable about membership of one. To share one's values, linguistic resources or history with others may conduce to valued relationships with them, but then any value one's consequent cultural identity may have is parasitic upon this communal one; and it may be less valuable for one than a communal identity not so supported by common cultural characteristics – for example, from membership of a multicultural neighbourhood. In fact it may not be valuable for one at all if it stands in the way of such other claims upon one.

The arguments I have looked at so far have been instrumentalist in the sense that they have asked what value a cultural identity might have for an individual in terms of his or her psychological functioning, where this includes social functioning as a part of dealings with the world generally. There is an aspect to this which we need to mention, however, before turning to a related non-instrumentalist argument. It is that a cultural identity might be valuable for a person in enabling her to be 'placed', as we say, by others and responded to confidently and, perhaps, appropriately. Now, depending upon what this response to it is, such a cultural identity may be valuable for someone in smoothing their social path, or it may be detrimental if it provokes an adverse reaction. No general judgement can be returned, although, it may be claimed, at least within one's own cultural group, the identity will be valuable. But even here we can raise a criticism similar to previous ones, for it is not clear that this kind of cosy fitting into a group is really valuable for someone if it militates against the flexibility that a multicultural environment demands. And it must be noted, finally, that the cultural identity whose value may be argued for along the lines we are considering need only be a surface identity, since nothing deep is needed for responses to be made to someone in virtue of their presumed cultural identity, only rough conformity to a stereotype.

This instrumentalist argument, however, is related to one that finds an intrinsic value in having a cultural identity of the group membership sort we are considering. It is that a clear cultural identity, by contrast with a cosmopolitan mixture of cultural elements, gives someone's personality – which might otherwise be amorphous – a definite form. It is not just that people find it manageable, but that they value it ethically and aesthetically – ethically because it is firm and orderly, aesthetically because comprehensible and uncomplicated. Yet it seems to be begging the question, perhaps owing to functionalist assumptions, that such properties belong to cultural identities and not to isolated individual ones. Nor is it obvious that these properties are intrinsically more valuable than their ethical and aesthetic opposites of suppleness and complexity. Artistic and literary representations of cultural types are likely to have biased our judgements here.

A Need for Identity?

Perhaps the biggest confusion in much writing about the value of cultural identity is that between ascribing it value *for* the individual and attributing it a value *to* her. Writers often move seamlessly between the two as if they came to much the same thing, but, while the principal point of arguments from the value of identity for people is to show how the supposed depth of the identity justifies certain political arrangements without which they would be threatened with a variety of malfunctions, all that the claim that an identity is important to people can justify is that withholding recognition and its political concomitants demeans them or otherwise does not give them their due, failing to give weight to their own valuations. This is a much less powerful conclusion, since it may not be accepted that what they take to be their due is in fact due to them; for it is a common observation that people often expect more than they have any right to by thinking of various features of themselves as more important than they are – their looks, their intellect, or whatever. Why should the same not be true of some identity?

What this rhetorical question brings out is that whereas for identity to have a value for people it would only be necessary that they had it, for it to be valuable to them they thus must think of themselves as having it. They must, that is to say, make this self-identification, which does not, of course, require any deep identity, nor, indeed, need it correspond to anything that goes deep with them. The self-identification having been made, however, what is taken to be the identity's value *to* the individual? It is variously supposed to be of value because it confers a sense of identity, self-respect, identification with others, endorsement by them and so on. But it will not surprise readers of earlier chapters to learn that this seems to me to take the cultural identity whose various values to individuals are so itemised to be a unitary phenomenon, while I have argued that we have several distinct types of identity here, even if they are combinable. And with each of the different types goes a different value to the individual who professes the identity.

Herder, as we have seen, believed that there were radical differences between people of different cultures. To have a sense of who they were, therefore, they needed to grasp how they were different from others, what made them the distinct sort of people they were. But he saw these differences as especially marked out in differences of language, customs, music and art – not, of course, in the productions of elites who have been tainted by exposure to foreign models, but in folk customs, folk stories, folk music *und so weiter*. It is in such a language and through such forms that one can express one's own distinctness, because, as Avishai Margalit puts it, 'The idea is that people make use of different styles to express their humanity . . . There are people who express themselves "Frenchly", while others have forms of life that are expressed "Koreanly" or "Syrianly" or "Icelandically".'[5] The type of identity being expressed here is what I earlier referred to as identity as face – the adoption of a persona that conspicuously differentiates someone from those of another culture. What, then, is the value to people of an identity as face?

Herder himself believed that there is a universal human need to express oneself – literally to express who one is. This, for Romantics who followed him, is the task of creative artists. But it is also supposedly a drive in others, and since one's cultural identity is part of who one is, it is a drive to express, to externalise, this identity. Only as so externalised, in fact, is it fully realised as an identity. This is not the place to treat the pathologies of Romanticism which continue to motivate consumption under capitalism; only to observe that their ubiquity makes it easy to exploit them in the service of culturalist and nationalist politics, so that in employing distinctive cultural markers members will see what they are doing as expressing themselves and attach value to it for this reason. The value to them of cultural identity as face, then, will be, at least in part, its value as self-expression.

It should by now go without saying that I discern no universal need of the kind from whose satisfaction this value is supposed to derive, nor the prior existence of those cultural groupings whose boundaries are marked by their members' expressions of distinctness. There is nothing to 'express' – to bring out from within – here and no need to express anything. There is only the collective creation or articulation of recognisable difference, sometimes on the basis of differences ascribed by others, sometimes by generalising, simplifying or prioritising convenient markers of difference. But the motive for this, I have argued, is a social or political need for dissociation in particular circumstances – circumstances, that is to say, that are by no means universal, but which are such as to pose the threat of assimilation, cultural domination and the like. In Herder's time it was the perceived threat of French cultural influences in Germany and the attempts by the empires of his day to unify disparate peoples. Yet these are local situations provoking predictable responses, not, as he took them to be, examples of a natural spirit of difference being thwarted.

Similarly the idea that cultural identity is valuable to people because it confers self-respect or self-esteem seems to me to have primary application to what I called identity as standing, and this type of identity is a reaction to being despised or undervalued by others. No doubt there is in some sense a universal need for self-respect, but it is far from clear either that this has to be experienced when one's cultural or national group is disvalued or that the need should be satisfied by cultural identification. Members of the working class, to take an analogous case, are commonly despised by the middle classes, but they have not typically reacted by a collective class identification which valorises their life and outlook, to the despair of Marxists. They have just ignored it. Though cultural identity as standing is a reaction to another culture's disdain, it is far from an inevitable one and it depends upon other political factors to be actuated in response to any perceived need. These complex factors, such as the individual humiliation or disregard of political elites, are drawn upon to create a general sense of need. There is no reason to think that any such need predates them.

Conversely, then, there is no reason to suppose that cultural identification can suitably fulfil a general need for self-respect. Some people take pride in their culture or nation, others simply make an identification with it without any such feelings or, indeed, with contrary ones. Whether such an identity is of value to them depends upon their overall value system and is not some additional free-floating value, as much writing on this subject seems to suggest. Thus many people find self-respect not in cultural identity, but in family membership, profession, civic role and so forth, and they have no need for more. Indeed, we are rightly disparaging of jingoists, for example, whose self-worth derives primarily from membership of a nation. And not all nations or other cultural groups are such that membership of them ought to be a source of pride; for they may be in various ways seriously deserving of censure: ill formed, ill-disposed or otherwise unworthy. The value of such an identity to their members is delusory.

The need to belong is a third human requisite whose satisfaction by membership of a culture or nation, and its corresponding identity, is said by many authors to be of value to people. For example, Bhikhu Parekh takes Samuel Huntington to maintain that 'the quest for cultural identity is a central human concern. It involves asking who we are, where we belong and feel most at home, what we stand for, and how we should organise our individual and collective lives.'[6] Others associate the belonging supposedly needed with a sort of association with others that is not based on achievement and thus allows spontaneous behaviour because one feels at home with them.[7] Here the family is cited as the paradigm, and those who follow Herder in thinking of the nation as an extended family regard cultural membership as analogous to belonging to a family. There are, however, two distinct ideas here, corresponding to two types of identity I described earlier.

The first is the idea of belonging as a cure for rootlessness, for homelessness in the sense of not having a place, literal or metaphysical, which one can think of as one's own. The type of identity which is a reaction to the threat of this rootlessness is what I called identity as home. So the value of this cultural identity to people would be that it provides them with their own place. The notion that there is a universal human need to belong in this way seems to me to be an unjustified deduction from the fact that certain circumstances do lead to feelings of insecurity which are articulated in terms of these images of homelessness and so on. Sometimes people who experience them have literally lost their homes, been uprooted from their original place; at others they have been exposed to rapid change or other circumstances that loosen established ties. But it does not follow from this that those unaffected by such factors actually feel at home and in doing so satisfy some basic need. Rather, such feelings arise when contrary feelings threaten. This is not entirely to deny the value of the identities that sustain them to those who are thrust into circumstances of this sort of homelessness. But it is, of course, no substitute for material improvements in their situation. The notion that finding comfort in cultural identity is a response to 'a central human concern' is in danger of masking this simple fact.

The other idea of belonging for which a general need is claimed is that supplied by what I called identity as affiliation, which is a reaction to feeling alone and unconnected to others. Doubtless we all do need such connections, which are normally to be formed among family and friends. The sorts of circumstance in which these seem insufficient are those that make people feel, as the phrase goes, alone in a crowd, and they include migration, urbanisation and rejection by others. The value of cultural identity to those in these circumstances is to provide relief from such feelings of loneliness. But again, I suggest, they are only a substitute for what is really needed. Based, as it is, on the presumption that one can have the needed connections with those who are like oneself, identity as affiliation may not in fact yield the relationships that provide a real refuge from isolation. The assumption that it does depends on the confusion noted earlier between cultural identity and community membership. What might really be of value is the latter.

It is, I suspect, the assimilation of culture to community that leads authors like Huntington, to move easily from taking 'the quest for cultural identity' to involve 'asking . . . where we belong and feel most at home' to its leading us to question 'what we stand for, and how we should organise our individual and collective lives'. The assumption here seems to be that we belong to a community and feel at home there, and, as a result, discover the values we should live by in those of the community. Now, certainly a community requires a set of rules for its social interactions, but to know them is not something of value to its members: it is simply a necessary condition of their participating in the community. To grasp such a set of rules, however, is a very different thing from adhering to certain ethical ideals, while to have such ideals is what can be of value to someone in giving her something to 'stand for'. Communities, though, do not require any such ideals. Rather, what offer ideals are cultures defined in terms of values – those cultures membership of which provide what I called identity as centre. The value to members of this type of identity is, as I put it, to fill the gap that the threat of hollowness would open up in circumstances which cast into doubt the existence of values to live by individually or collectively.

I have already questioned whether identity as centre actually does provide such values or only statements of them demanding notional assent. The latter could, of course, considerably influence behaviour and whether a cultural identity founded on such an assent is really valuable depends upon whether the values in question are worthwhile ones. Analogously, it might be added, the real value of a cultural identity as mission depends upon what that mission is, though the value individuals find in it will lie in its offering them a shared purpose. There are, I want to reiterate, distinct notions involved here, though ones it is easy to confuse when thinking in terms of how people organise their lives. That said, it is also important to realise that in the right combined circumstances these different types of identity, as others, can be amalgamated. This is no reason to think, however, that all cultural identities are taken to be of value to members in all the different ways I have mentioned. It depends, I have claimed, on the type of identity involved and that is determined by the circumstances of its formation. So the value members of a group now set on their cultural identity may have come to be divorced from any value it might have had in those circumstances, and just derive from the way it has been constructed. This is yet another reason to make us sceptical about the value of cultural identity.

The Disvalue of Identity

There are a number of stock objections to the politics of cultural identity which must now be considered if we are to go on to assess the *disvalue* of cultural identification. Two of these are that, on the one hand, cultural identity imposes a false unity upon those to whom it is assigned and, on the other, that it creates false dichotomies between those assigned different identities.[8] I believe these two objections apply more to some types of identity than to others, rather than constituting general criticisms of the process of identity construction along cultural lines. For example, identity as affiliation in the way that I have characterised, demands a high degree of sameness of group members, particularly in the way they live their lives, for this is taken to be needed for the community or solidarity they seek to establish or preserve through endorsing the identity. Here, internal differences are a threat. Groups like the Amish may provide examples of these. Identity as face, by contrast, permits a considerable range of internal variation so long as the conspicuous markers of difference from those outside the group are preserved. But identity as face does tend to divide people sharply and hence obscure common interests. Identities marked by language, as in the case of the Québecois, exemplify this, and in such situations nation-building across linguistic differences can be fraught.

I do not maintain that the phenomena to which the two objections draw our attention are witnessed only with these types of identity. But in other cases they may be the result of the content of identities. Identity as centre, for instance, may involve normative content that tends to homogenise group members, as with indigenous peoples who follow a warrior ethic. On the other hand, it may valorise internal diversity, as with the supposed English love of liberty which celebrates eccentrics. Again, some values in identities as centre work to exclude outsiders, as Western political culture values democracy in opposition to dictatorship (stifling questions about the nature of that democracy), and thereby demonises those who support authoritarian regimes, perhaps sometimes for good Hobbesian reasons. By contrast, French political culture, at least in its republican form, was taken to have a wide normative appeal, with the mixed blessing that colonial subjects who grasped it might find themselves incorporated into metropolitan France.

Some other reservations about the politics of cultural identity do relate to the character of such identities more generally. Thus it is argued that they present a 'danger of freezing or naturalizing a historically acquired identity';[9]

and this is related to the objection that they 'undermine the possibility of critical reflection' through members becoming 'engulfed' in the group,[10] for in each case the thought is that the identity represented by their membership may not be appropriate to the circumstances they are actually in. This complaint has a good deal of justification, as I indicated at the end of the last section. Cultural identities are commodities often consumed long after their sell-by dates with adverse consequences. Although they can change, as I earlier observed, both in type and in content to suit new conditions, this normally requires political intervention. Otherwise they will continue to carry the imprint of the circumstances of their construction. In the case of identity as standing, to take one example, this can lead to posturing and resentment long after the occasion for them has passed. The typical attitude of many Germans in the first half of the twentieth century illustrates this point.

Rather than dwell on these criticisms familiar in the literature, I want to develop some others. The first is that identity politics leads to pessimism about the possibilities of political concord between people who seem or think of themselves as different. I want to cast doubt on an argument sometimes used for the recognition of cultural identities construed in terms of shared values, or rather – for here the boundary-marking role of such values is indeed acknowledged – in terms of values not shared by others. The argument is that those with widely conflicting values need to be recognised as ethically different sorts of people, and that political arrangements should be made accordingly. The picture behind such claims, if not the claims themselves, is one espoused by, for example, Stuart Hampshire,[11] following in the footsteps of Berlin. People define themselves in opposition to others and therefore want to preserve their cultural distinctiveness, Hampshire maintains. This distinctiveness is exemplified in contrasting ethical ideals which are the products of different imaginations. But because imagination is different in different peoples, cultural diversity is 'an essential and deep feature of human nature',[12] and it leads to conflict about how life should be led, goods distributed and so on. 'Conflict is perpetual,' affirms Hampshire in Heraclitean mode, 'why should we be deceived?'[13]

It is, according to this account, self-deceiving to imagine there is a common human nature. Instead we are invited to think of radically different natures corresponding to distinct cultural identities. It is not least this alleged correspondence that we should question. Perhaps there are some relatively isolated societies with fairly homogeneous ethical cultures whose members are recognisably similar in their moral reactions and different in them from the members of other societies. The difference between Athenians and Spartans provides a tempting model for this. But such societies are by no means typical of our contemporary world. Members of different societies are usually exposed through the media to each others' cultures and to other common cultural influences. Nor are cultures at all homogeneous in the sense that all members pursue similar ideals. Saints and heroes present ideals within a single society as different as any that may be found between them. There is, though, a slide in this argument which renders it highly suspect. Saints and heroes are different kinds of people, not different identities in any sense antecedent to their equation with practical identities.[14] Only if different cultural identities carried with them analogous differences of character or aspiration would the argument stand up, and that is what may be questioned for very many of the cultural groups on behalf of which claims backed by this sort of argument are raised. To equate identity with practical identity here is a tactical move, but one that needs support beyond the merely stipulative that it seldom or never receives.

No doubt a society that makes possible a range of lifestyles to suit different sorts of people is, for a variety of reasons, better than one which does not, though doubtless too there are limits on what range is possible (and in any society many people find themselves square pegs in round holes). This is, of course, a very different matter from postulating different sorts of society for different sorts of people, as some political claims may demand. Different sorts of society, different ways of life, may, it might be suggested, produce different sorts of people, so that the identities corresponding to membership of them, with their different cultures, do correlate with different sorts of people. But then being in a monastery or serving in the army might equally produce different sorts of people and no political claims follow. It is not possible to make identity claims do the work they would need to do on these sorts of grounds. For there is no reason to think that different sorts of people cannot live harmoniously together in the same society. And, in general, a plurality of conflicting values, some prioritised by some people, others by others, is a situation that has to be coped with within any society. It is, so far, wrongheaded to suppose that practical identities different in this way need to be accommodated in different societies and, therefore, that whatever argument a cultural group may have for such separation, it is not strengthened by claiming a distinctive practical identity for its members.

This tells against such typical manifestations of the politics of identity as opposition to immigration based on claims of cultural incompatibility where this is given in terms of psychological differences, rather than, say, differences in practices which may cause friction. But it tells equally against both the idea that the integration of immigrants is difficult or impossible because it confronts deep psychological obstacles arising from a distinct value-culture identity, and the notion that what should be demanded of immigrants is a change in identity conceived in such terms. Yet it is just this latter sort of demand, explicit or implicit, that characteristically leads immigrant groups to seek special political arrangements to preserve their identities, as they might express it. Seeing themselves as different, not least because treated as such by the indigenous population, they claim special educational provision, for example, or even group representation or various types of autonomy. Yet while they may well have good grounds for expecting their language or religious needs to be treated in the same way as those of their adoptive country, and perhaps specific political arrangements will be needed to ensure this, none of that implies any right to separate treatment based on a different identity.

A criticism closely related to the one I have been discussing is that attachment to identities constructed in terms of values or world views actually endangers the compromises necessary for harmonious co-existence and leads to extremism. The idea of cultural values as part of a deep identity fosters the belief that a deliberate change in one's ideals or evaluations, perhaps in response to novel experiences or new associations, is somehow difficult or disreputable. For if such things are really part, a constitutive part, of what one is, then one would have to change what one is, become a different person, to accomplish this change. That makes it seem a daunting task, while in fact, of course, people make these changes frequently and often easily. We may be right to criticise people who do it *too* easily as superficial and impressionable, but that is because we expect such matters to be important to people, so that they should seek a certain consistency in, and thereby be able to take responsibility for, what they believe to be right or find desirable. None of that adds up to criticising them for being untrue to themselves, as the idea that major changes in such beliefs would involve a lack of integrity implies. Any criticism of a person to that effect might be matched by criticism of others, who do not change, as rigid or inflexible, perhaps out of blindness to other options or from anxiety in the face of them. Identity talk in this area grossly oversimplifies the range of possibilities.

I am led to conclude, then, that the notion of a value culture identity, in the sense that I have given it, is of little or no application, and cannot serve to justify the sort of political claims it is called upon to support. It is also pernicious in limiting our thinking about people and tends to produce in them politically unprofitable attitudes. Constructing cultural identity in terms of values is, I claim, morally and politically harmful. The key point is that if values are thought of as a part of one's identity then a failure to realise such values is necessarily conceived of as a failure to be oneself, a betrayal of who one is. The mechanism for realising the supposedly shared values of a cultural group, then, is to inculcate this kind of sentiment in its members. The upshot of achieving this is, I suggest, necessarily an extremist politics in which the single-minded pursuit of political goals that realise the values of the group is dictated by the maintenance of its members' identity.

Extremism, as I understand it here, contrasts with moderation – or 'trimming', as it used to be known, in virtue of the way in which a boat is prevented from capsizing as a result of placing too much weight in one side by putting some weight on the other. Moderates, then, adopt the unprincipled-looking expedient of giving weight to a variety of values in order not to run the risks associated with pursuing a single set, namely a loss of stability and an adverse reaction from those with other values. Moderation would not, I want to argue, be readily open to value culture groups, for if their values are to be constitutive of individual identities then they must, psychologically, be internally fixed and harmonious, not admitting of radical disjunctures, for this would upset someone's sense of who she really was. Yet it is just such disjunctures, between, for example, freedom and order, that moderates believe need to be balanced out in order to achieve stable and peaceable political arrangements.

There are two kinds of consequence that follow from this diagnosis, differing in whether they are largely independent of or depend upon intergroup relations. The first kind simply exhibits the dangers of the zealous pursuit of a limited range of ethical ideals. The attempt to impose upon American society generally the values of the religious right as constitutive of American identity exemplifies this in its potential to polarise and destabilise US society. So too, of course, does the not dissimilar drive to prescribe supposedly Muslim values for all the people of largely pious Islamic states and perhaps beyond. In each case there is a degree of intolerance, but not necessarily so much of other values regarded as constitutive of other alternative identities, as of attitudes and actions regarded as not qualifying to count as ethical at all. This type of situation is illustrated by many instances of the political imperative to realise the values claimed to be constitutive of 'Western' identity – freedom, political equality, democracy and so on. For example, armed intervention in states that clearly do not demonstrate regard for these values, whether justified in terms of humanitarian objectives or regime change, is presented as a duty incumbent on those who profess them, often ignoring other values – order, respect and so forth – which might be counterposed to them in the interests of peace.

The second kind of potentially adverse consequence of an identity politics couched in terms of values is noted by Daniel Weinstock, who argues that it militates against compromise with those who profess differing values and hence conduces to conflict.[15] A compromise will be perceived as a loss of integrity by both parties, since neither of their opposing values can be realised in it. Weinstock adds that, while interests can be partially satisfied in compromise arrangements, identity-constituting values cannot; and, while interest claims are empirically testable, those based on identity-constituting values are not, thereby reducing the scope for discussion and accommodation. In fact the situation seems rather worse then even Weinstock imagines in his attack upon identity politics. For if principled agreement does depend upon an appeal to values shared between the parties then to the extent to which two cultural groups' values are opposed they are likely to regard such agreement as unobtainable and therefore resort to non-deliberative and possibly violent means to attain their objectives. But if cultural groups are constructed in terms of contrasts with other relevant groups then at least a large range of values in terms of which they are constructed will be opposed to those of these other groups. This seems to be a recipe for political conflict unless the groups operate in separate political spheres. It is also, I maintain, morally harmful. For it is the moral duty of citizens of a state, for example, to pursue policies that do not unnecessarily engender conflict within it, and of international statesmen to work, wherever possible, for peace. To appreciate the duties of such roles and of what is required to fulfil them is, if I am right, incompatible with entering politics in an identity constructed through membership of a value culture.

This kind of criticism does not apply only to identities constructed in terms of value. There may be nothing wrong in the appropriate circumstances with constructing identities in terms of a shared language but the metaphysical inflation of this into a story of a shared world view has evident dangers, especially if linked to the thesis that different world views are incommensurable. For if a group believes it has a world view not shared by others then it will, to this extent, regard political negotiations with other groups as difficult or impossible when each side sees the situation they concern quite differently. One might think here, for example, of the characteristically different ways in which indigenous peoples and settler groups view land and its suitability for exploitation. So long as this difference is regarded as constituted by widely divergent world views incorporated into the different languages that separate these groups then the sort of disputes that arise in such situations may seem rationally insoluble. The position is even worse when one, more powerful, group treats the alternative viewpoint with contempt and enforces its own preferred outcome, as if rational engagement is impossible until the other group is acculturated through the acquisition of a new language and thereby loses, or renders inoperative, its old identity. Such attitudes, endemic in this view of cultural identity, lead to oppression and conflict.

To say that these are avoidable is not to deny that there may be different viewpoints on such matters which are hard to bridge. But the remedy does not lie in some act of recognising distinct identities that give rise to them. That is exactly what could not lead to a rational resolution of disputes, but, at best, some division of spheres within which the distinct identity groups operate. Rather, the remedy lies in an attempt to understand and appreciate the other's viewpoint, while remaining sceptical of its supposed irrevocability precisely because one denies its link to identity. Nor, correspondingly, is one's attempt threatened by, or threatening to, one's own putative perspectival identity. It is attempts at understanding of this sort that are incumbent on those whose roles are concerned with the peaceable settlement of disputes. Any conceptualisation of their position which hinders them, as does the notion of cultural identity under discussion, is to be deprecated.

I have suggested that a politics of cultural identity stands unnecessarily in the way of the rational resolution of disagreements and leads to discord. But the situation is, in fact, much worse than this. For the claims that are made on the basis of cultural identities are seldom rationally determinable because they conflict with each other, and because this conflict is the result of identity groups being constructed in accordance with incompatible criteria. Thus, the fact that identities are overlapping, far from being the answer to the tendency to essentialise them that some claim, creates its own insoluble problems. The classic example is the conflict between the identities associated with existing states and those of separatist groups.

In the break up of Yugoslavia, for example, it was principally religious differences which were supposed to distinguish Serb from Croat. This is a distinction based on a value culture conception, not because Catholics and Orthodox embrace very divergent values, but because these churches represent different attachments. This value culture distinction could be supplemented by a chronicle culture one, since Serbia and Croatia had distinct political histories until 1918 and during the Second World War. Such criteria conflict with a language culture one, since both Serbs and Croats speak Serbo-Croat. It is true that there are differences in the language they speak, and different scripts are used for writing it, though these were closely associated with the religious difference. And in fact, there is a mosaic of dialects throughout the Serbo-Croat speaking parts of the former Yugoslavia, so that just as Serbo-Croat was fashioned to unify its members, now Serbian and Croatian are being shaped to divide them.

What do such conflicting criteria for cultural identity imply? That depends upon what claims are being based upon it. In the Yugoslav case it is the right to separate statehood, which is the characteristic claim of supposedly national cultures – indeed, arguably, the claim that picks them out as national. But since states form a system of non-overlapping territorial units the conflict in criteria for national identity is fatal, and makes the principled and pacific resolution of national claims to separate statehood impossible. Without consistent and agreed criteria there will be intractable disagreements over what territorial units should be states. This not only threatens discord and violence between the parties in conflict; a group that bases its claim to statehood on its language, say, even if that claim has already been realised, ought not to recognise the legitimacy of other states not so grounded, just as it would not recognise the legitimacy of such a state when, if its claim was unrecognised, it sought to secede from it. But this would be a recipe for international chaos and disharmony. Fortunately pragmatic considerations incline those who think of themselves as nations against treating putative imposters to this title in this way. But by the same token it is hard to suppress a doubt that nationalist arguments propounded for a right to statehood may not themselves be tactical rather than principled.

However, we should notice that the impossibility of a principled resolution of national claims applies to others based on putative cultural identities. Consider claims for group representation in democratic systems, advocated for a variety of marginalised groups, including minority cultures, by, for example, Iris Marion Young.[16] Yet, if such cultural groups are conceived now in terms of religion, now language, now history and now community, as might plausibly be supposed for various immigrant and indigenous groups, a scheme of group representation will work equitably only if these groups are disjoint in their membership. If there are overlaps then those at the intersections of groups will be, in a certain sense, over-represented. Young herself might reply that she picks out groups in terms of their distinctive perspectives – by which she seemingly means something more general than shared opinions and attitudes but less restrictive than a shared language. Rather, they are the perspectives of those with shared experiences, in particular of disadvantage. It is, though, very difficult to see how this criterion could in practice be applied to identify the groups to be democratically represented.

Similar considerations apply if cultural identity groups claim to run their own affairs in anything other than the narrowest sense in which, say, religious groups run their own religions or language groups might have some control over their languages, how they are to be taught, enriched poetically and so forth. But if identity groups claim a right to control access to what they regard as their own space or the behaviour of non-members within it, then, unless they are disjoint, irresolvable conflicts can arise. Or groups differently constituted may claim to control members' behaviour in various aspects, for example in relation to marriage or education, and again there may be no principled way to determine whose writ should run. In each case the reason for the impasse is that the claims are presented as arising from the identities of members, as needed in some way to maintain or secure these claims. But what constitute the real or primary identities of those concerned is precisely what the appeal to conflicting criteria makes undecidable. It is, to repeat, the justification of these claims through the appeal to a putative true identity, together with the apparent absence of a way of determining this, which in the above cases creates rationally irresolvable oppositions.

Conclusion

My criticisms of the politics of cultural identity may leave the impression of a marked lack of sympathy for the situation of cultural minorities and of support for established states however unsympathetic they are themselves. Yet that is not my position. It is only that the politics of identity is not the best way to tackle the problems of groups that are oppressed or discriminated against, inevitable as it may be – given the prevailing *Weltanschauung* – that this is how they will be conceptualised. Rather, I believe that, instead of identities, real material interests should be acknowledged and arrangements made to serve them. What these interests are is often implicit in the way a putative cultural identity is constructed. A minority language, to take an obvious example, can put its speakers at a disadvantage in employment, participation in public affairs and so forth. Efforts need to be made to minimise these effects by normalising its use wherever possible, including, where appropriate, granting autonomy and language protection provisions to territorially concentrated language groups.

What stands in the way of such an approach is often identity politics itself, as embraced by the majority. Assimilationist demands upon immigrants, for example, often have this character, claiming that the majority language must be used because this is the language of the nation and hence a necessary qualification for membership of it. But such conceptions get in the way of debating how to accommodate minority language speakers on the basis that they are simply fellow residents. It is in this role, I suggest (which is the basis for a more substantial citizenship), that members of the majority and minority should come together to address the problems. Of course there are relations of unequal power here, but it is precisely to mitigate their impact that the role is assumed. For being a fellow resident of a place puts one under an obligation to consider the problems others might face in living together with one in it, so that imaginatively I can conceive of myself as having the same problems and wanting to have them taken account of. (Consider a majority language speaker in an immigrant ghetto.) Not to think in this way is to refuse to accept the role, but the circumstances surely dictate that this is the role one should assume.

Exchanges within roles such as these can be intercultural so long as all parties understand the requirements of the role in the same way. Of course there may be misunderstandings and differences in expectations, but there should be no a priori reason to think that these are somehow incapable of being overcome. It is only versions of the politics of cultural identity that lead to such damaging conclusions, as I indicated in discussing the ways in which identity politics militates against compromise. Whether or not public reason can be conducted without reliance on specific cultural values,[17] it is the capacity and willingness to engage in such reasoning that characterises the role of citizen. And it is in this role that one must ask what is best for citizens as a whole, advancing one's own interests within this context rather than in some narrower one in which one occupies a more restricted position. It is hard to see, then, that group representation and the like, as advanced by proponents of identity politics, could work within such a framework, unless it was simply to ensure that some specific interest were heard, and thereafter for the general interest to be addressed.

There is no guarantee that any particular collective approach to problem solving will work to mollify those who are aggrieved at how they are treated. In these circumstances there need be no presumption in favour of preserving the political status quo. Again it is usually a majoritarian identity politics that stands in the way of changes in the direction of political separation or other remedies. But secession on the grounds of oppression or discrimination is a very different thing from secession on national grounds.[18] The former may be justified if no agreed accommodation can be reached, while, if I am right, there are no good arguments for the latter on the basis of claims to a distinctive cultural identity.

Notes

1. See especially, Will Kymlicka, *Multicultural Citizenship* (Oxford: Oxford University Press, 1995).
2. Cp. Bhikhu Parekh, *Rethinking Multiculturalism* (Basingstoke: Macmillan, 2000), ch. 3.
3. Charles Taylor, *Philosophical Arguments* (Cambridge, MA: Harvard University Press, 1997), p. 140.
4. Kymlicka, *Multicultural Citizenship*, pp. 82–3.
5. Avishai Margalit, 'The moral psychology of nationalism', in R. McKim and J. McMahan (eds), *The Morality of Nationalism* (New York, NY: Oxford University Press, 1997), p. 84.
6. Bhikhu Parekh, *A New Politics of Identity* (Basingstoke: Palgrave Macmillan, 2008), p. 153.
7. E.g. Margalit, 'The moral psychology'.

8. Cp. Parekh, *A New Politics*, p. 35.
9. Ibid. p. 36.
10. Andrew Mason, *Community, Solidarity and Belonging* (Cambridge: Cambridge University Press, 2000), p. 57.
11. See Stuart Hampshire, *Justice is Conflict* (London: Duckworth, 1999).
12. Ibid. p. 43.
13. Ibid. p. 51.
14. E.g. Matthew Festenstein, *Negotiating Diversity* (Cambridge: Polity, 2005), ch. 1.
15. Daniel Weinstock, 'Is "identity" a danger to democracy?', in I. Primoratz and A. Pavkovic (eds), *Identity, Self-Determination and Secession* (Aldershot: Ashgate, 2006).
16. Iris Marion Young, *Inclusion and Democracy* (Oxford: Oxford University Press, 2000), ch. 4.
17. As John Rawls holds it should: *Political Liberalism* (New York, NY: Columbia University Press, 1996), lecture VI.
18. I develop this distinction in *Peoples, Cultures and Nations* (Edinburgh: Edinburgh University Press, 2000), ch. 9.

Index

Index

Gellner, E., 83, 140–1
Geordies, 3
Germans/Germany, 19, 28–30, 33, 49–50, 68, 70–3, 100, 126, 180, 186
Goering, H., 1
Greeks (ancient), 17–19, 23, 79, 167
group representation, 11, 195–6, 198
gypsies, 135; *see also* Roma

Habermas, J., 132, 136
habitus, 144–6
Hampshire, S., 186–7
Hegel, G. W. F., 30, 41, 133, 140
Heidegger, M., 29, 167–8, 170
Heraclitus, 30, 187
Herder, J. G. von, 19, 28–9, 36, 39–42, 47, 60, 66–7, 73, 81, 92, 170, 173–4, 179–81
history, 20–1, 26, 42, 56–7, 60, 64, 81, 85, 87, 89, 174, 176, 195
home, identity as, 84–7, 89, 104–5, 107–8, 112, 115, 117, 182
Honneth, A., 75
Hume, D., 17
Huntington, S., 181, 183

idealism, 25–7, 30, 33–4, 38
ideology, 130–2, 139–43
immigrants/immigration, 7, 38, 79, 86, 107–9, 117
individual identity, 2–3, 5–6, 43–8, 177
Ireland/Irish, 54, 56, 62–3, 77, 82, 113, 152–71, 175
Islam, 42, 72–3, 107, 120–1, 191; *see also* Muslims
Israel, 87

Japanese, 103, 107
Jews, 29, 40, 87

Kant, I., 28, 66, 162, 166, 168–70
Kedourie, E., 29
Kidd, B., 27–8
Klein, M., 130–2
Kohlberg, L., 131
Kristeva, J., 124–5, 134–8

Kukathas, C., 12
Kurds, 8
Kymlicka, W., 10, 12–13, 60–1, 174–6

label, identity as, 91
Lacan, J., 133–4
language, 20, 22, 29, 39–42, 46–7, 52–5, 60–2, 64, 68–9, 73, 78, 80, 83, 86, 107, 114, 120–2, 133–4, 138, 153–60, 174–6, 179, 185, 189, 192–3, 195–7
language culture, 52–5
Laski, H., 33–5
Le Bon, G., 125–6, 128–9
Levy, J., 12
liberalism/liberals, 10–13, 17, 27, 32, 131, 136, 139, 142, 174
Lindsay, A. D., 33–4

MacIver, R. M., 33–4
McDougall, W., 24, 31, 126–8
McGarry, J., 129
MacLiammóir, M., 153
Malayans, 98–9
Margalit, A., 179
Marx, K., 138–43
materialism, 26–7
Maugham, W. Somerset, 21, 31
Maurras, C., 29
Mazzini, J., 88
Meinecke, F., 27
Merleau-Ponty, M., 99, 101–3, 107
Mill, J. S., 20, 27, 32, 34
Miller, D., 66–7, 129, 137
mission, identity as, 87–90, 184
moderation, 190
Mohanty, S., 64
Moore, G., 161
music, 86, 89, 152, 160–5, 179
Muslims, 48, 51–2, 63, 72–3, 80–1, 90, 95–112, 117, 120–2, 191; *see also* Islam

narrative identity, 46–7, 56, 64
national character, 13, 16–36, 38–9, 43, 49, 72, 75–6, 87, 92, 112, 139
nationalism/nationalists, 8, 10, 12, 19–23, 27, 29, 32, 35, 52, 57, 66–70, 73, 132, 137, 140, 142, 153, 195
Nietzsche, F., 29